Especially for Mother

Especially
for Mother

AN AFFECTIONATE ANTHOLOGY

VANCE HYDE

Established 1834

New York · THOMAS Y. CROWELL COMPANY

ACKNOWLEDGMENTS

For permission to reprint copyrighted material, grateful acknowledgment is extended to the following:

Dorothy Aldis for "Woman at Window," reprinted by permission of *Good Housekeeping Magazine*.

Appleton-Century Crofts, Inc., for material from *How to Be a Happy Woman* by Ardis Whitman.

Alan Beck for "What Is a Boy?" and "What Is a Girl?" copyright by the New England Mutual Life Insurance Co., and "What Is a Mother?"

Gladys Bell for "The Perfect Moment," copyright 1957 by the Reader's Digest Association, Inc. Reprinted with permission.

The Bell Syndicate, Inc., for "The Four-Year-Old Morning Child" by Katy Collins, from the column *Spousekeeping*.

Laura Berquist for material from "The American Woman: The New Mother and Housewife," reprinted from *Look Magazine*.

Brooke Byrne for "Evening News Flash," reprinted by permission of *Good Housekeeping Magazine*.

iv

Capper Publications, Topeka, Kansas, for "Song for a Husband" by Patricia M. Jordan.

Sara King Carleton for "Quite Contrary," reprinted by permission of *Good Housekeeping Magazine*.

Philip Jerome Cleveland for "Prayer for a New House," reprinted by permission of *Good Housekeeping Magazine*.

Elizabeth Coatsworth for "I Wish It Were April," reprinted by permission of *Good Housekeeping Magazine*.

Condé Nast Publications Inc. for "Where Is Peace," reprinted from *Vogue*, copyright 1947.

The Curtis Publishing Company for "Ingredients for Jam" by Mary Cooper, copyright 1949 The Curtis Publishing Company, "Every Child" by Edna Casler Joll, copyright 1943 The Curtis Publishing Company, and "Words for a Daughter" by Elizabeth Grey Stewart, copyright 1939 The Curtis Publishing Company.

Ethel Barnett de Vito for "Mother" and "The Letters," reprinted by permission of *Good Housekeeping Magazine*.

Dodd, Mead & Company for "How We Kept Mother's Day" by Stephen Leacock.

Glenn Ward Dresbach for "Late for Chores," reprinted by permission of *Good Housekeeping Magazine*.

E. P. Dutton & Co., Inc., for "After School" from *Singing Drums* by Helen Welshimer.

Norma Millay Ellis for "An Ancient Gesture" by Edna St. Vincent Millay, from *Mine the Harvest*, Harper & Brothers, copyright 1954 by Norma Millay Ellis.

Elaine V. Evans for "Reverie," "All You Have Loved," and "Mended Things," copyright 1949 The Curtis Publishing Company, and "Lost October," reprinted by permission of *Good Housekeeping Magazine*.

Ida Fasel for "Prayer for a New Daughter," reprinted by permission of *Good Housekeeping Magazine*.

Jessie Farnham for "Proposed Pact," reprinted by permission of *Good Housekeeping Magazine*.

Lulita Crawford Pritchett for "Mary Loved Lilacs," reprinted by permission of *Good Housekeeping Magazine*.

May Richstone for "Occupation: Housewife," reprinted by permission of *Good Housekeeping Magazine*.

Rinehart & Company for material from *Where Main Street Meets the River* by Hodding Carter, material from *The Disappearance* by Philip Wylie, and "Knitted Shawl" by Margaret Widdemer.

Margaret E. Sangster for "Letters from Camp," reprinted by permission of *Good Housekeeping Magazine*.

Charles Scribner's Sons for material from *A Diary of Private Prayer* by John Baillie.

Louise Shattuck for "Definition of a Mother."

Myrtle Vorst Sheppard for "God to a Mother," reprinted by permission of *Good Housekeeping Magazine*.

Lydel Sims for selection on page 30.

Polly Toland for "William Makes Good," copyright 1957 The Curtis Publishing Company.

The Viking Press, Inc., for "The Maid-Servant at the Inn" from *The Portable Dorothy Parker*, copyright 1927, 1944 by Dorothy Parker.

Willis Kingsley Wing for "Is Your Child an Open Book" by Louise Dickinson Rich, copyright 1957 by Woman's Day, Inc.

For
GEORGIA BAIRD HAYES
AND THORNTON HAYES
*whose love of poetry
has enriched so many lives*

PERSONAL ACKNOWLEDGMENTS

For the endless digging and checking involved in tracing the selections in the book, I am deeply grateful to Mr. Jerome Jacobs, Mrs. Edith Krebs, Mr. Walter Roeder, Mr. Paul Rooney, and Miss Jane Van Arsdale of the Grosvenor Reference Library, Buffalo, New York; to Mr. Howard Lamm of the Grosvenor Library's Music Department; to Miss Dolores Ray and Mrs. Ida Silk of the Buffalo and Erie County Public Library Children's Room, and to Miss Joan Davis, Mr. David Rittenhouse, Miss Matilda Sparenblack, and Mr. James Sweeny of that library's North Park Branch.

Grateful acknowledgment is also tendered to Doris Rechin, who typed the manuscript.

CONTENTS

Beginning Days

The only experience in life that lives up to the advance billing is having a baby! Graduation Day, your first Prom, even your wedding day, all contain the seeds of anticlimax, the nagging suspicion that after all the planning and dreaming there should be something . . . something more.

But having a baby! Nothing your mother or your best friend has ever told you can quite prepare you for that exhilarating instant when you suddenly realize that you're a mother.

It may happen when the white tile walls echo with the spine-tingling, heart-stopping birth cry of that small new person. Or the first time you stroke the warm fuzzy top of his head. And some of us take even longer than that to find the moment, but find it we do.

Perhaps, for you, it began long ago, when you first knew, with a stillness in your heart. A softness. A listening.

I WISH IT WERE APRIL

I wish it were springtime now,
I wish it were April,
with the rain dripping down from the trees
and my baby safe at my side.

I wish that the winter were over,
the snow and the waiting,
that waiting and childbirth were past
and withdrawn like a tide.

I wish I were lying in bed,
between the white linen,
with a flower or two on my table
and peace in my breast,

And the rain making songs at the window
in trickles of silver,
and the newborn child at my side
and my spirit at rest.

ELIZABETH COATSWORTH

Or the moment of really becoming a mother may happen in that last tension-charged hour before your baby is born. From the labor room window you watch the forsythia bending in the warm wind, or the pungent smoke of burning leaves sifting through the crisp fall dusk, and suddenly a veil lifts and you see the world in a new dimension. Only for an instant, but someday in the years ahead a cloud formation or a spray of yellow blossoms, an amber autumn evening or a soft dawn wind will shatter you with sudden emotion, and you will say to your child, as mothers have through all the ages, wonderingly, "It was just such a day as this when you were born." Who can create such a story of wonder, when one day I was not and then I was!

But suppose you weren't there at all when your child was born? Suppose there was the shrilling of a phone, and suddenly all the longing ended: "We have a little boy for you . . ." So much to do, then, so many things to be made ready in the room you had thought was ready all these months. And his first night in his new life; was it like this?

The house was already full of Christmas . . . when I wrote the letter that brought him to us, a tiny dark child in the middle of the night . . . a little silent bundle of woe, his eyes enormous, and he sucking desperately on a small thumb that seemed permanent in his mouth. I took off his coat and cap and held him close for a long time. He did not cry or speak. He was like a little animal, stricken to stone with fear. I have seen a baby rabbit stop like that in the field when the dogs came by.

I carried him upstairs and we undressed him and washed him and put him into the crib we brought down from the attic, and laid him there. Still there was not a word and still the thumb was in the mouth and great dark eyes stared at one face and then another. One by one the family went to bed and I sat there alone with the baby. I let the light burn low so that there would not be darkness and so that he might see me, and I sang a little to him now and again. Once or twice he began to sob softly, and then he put out his other hand, the one he could spare, and I took it and held it and after a long time he slept.

PEARL BUCK

5

One day I was not and then I was. But now that he—or she—is, what lies ahead? Grandmother predicted fortunes by the day of the week a child was born—remember?

Monday's child is fair of face,
Tuesday's child is full of grace,
Wednesday's child is full of woe,
Thursday's child has far to go.
Friday's child is loving and giving,
Saturday's child works hard for a living,
And the child that's born on Sabbath Day
Is fair and wise and good and gay.

See how simple it is to insure your child a long and happy life? Just avoid Wednesday and Saturday, work and woe. But would you really guarantee his happiness by eliminating "working hard for a living"? Or even, for that matter, by shielding him from woe?

FOR ROBERT, LEARNING

What shall I tell you
    On the day
The neighbor's children
    Go away,
The kitten grows
    And moves along,
The crickets cease
    Their summer song?

And how shall I make you
   Understand
That snowflakes melt
   Within the hand,
That skies are distant—
   Much too far
For any child
   To reach a star?

Oh, what ways
   Can I devise
To keep the dream dust
   In your eyes?
And should I find them,
   If I could . . .
Would it be wise?
   Would it be good?

MARJORIE LEE

If it is not ease and cloudless skies, then what is it that we want for this new life? For a girl, should we wish great beauty?

PRAYER FOR A NEW DAUGHTER

If it's all the same to You,

Let her face express
Calm and courtesy, and, when she speaks,
Shine with an inward shininess—
Not pretty, Lord.

May her hands hold no glove
To child or garden,

7

But be two tending shapes of love—
Not pretty; earth-scarred.

I hope she'll like the everyday,
Lark-simply; grow a funny bone,
A thoughtful side; learn to pray.

Oh, let her be a woman and a wife—
Not pretty, Lord. Nice.

IDA FASEL

We want so much for them, dream such dreams, and often we cannot give them nearly so much as we should like to give. But after all, how much does it really take to create a home?

Because of the housing shortage near the military base where he was stationed, a young doctor and his wife and three children had to live in cramped quarters in a hotel. A friend said to the doctor's six-year-old daughter, "Isn't it too bad that you don't have a home?"

"Oh, we have a home," the youngster replied quickly.

"We just don't have a house to put it in."

M. ELIZABETH LYNCH

Even the barest, poorest house can be a home, transformed by the love and determination of a mother.

8

Anna was Steve's little woman
Who labored bitterly enough
Making children of stern and tragic stuff
And a rapture that was hammered rough,
Spilling steel into their spines, yet keeping them
    wistful and human . . .
Anna had her work to do
With cooking and cleaning
And washing the window curtains white as new,
Washing them till they wore through:
For her the white curtains had a meaning—
And starching them white against the savage
    will
Of the grim dust belching incessantly out of the
    mill;
Soaking and scrubbing and ironing against that
    gritty reek
Until her head swam and her knees went weak
And she could hardly speak—
A terrible unbeaten purpose persisted:
Colour crying against a colourless world!
White against black at the windows flung up, un-
    furled!
Candles and candle light!
The flags of a lonely little woman twisted
Out of her hunger for cool clean beauty, her hunger
    for white!—
These were her banners and this was her fight!

No matter how tired she was, however she would
    ache
In every nerve, she must boil the meat and bake
The bread—and the curtains must go up white for
    Steve's sake!
One thing was certain:

9

That John and Stanley and Helen and Mary and the
    baby Steven
Must be kept out of the mills and the mill life, even
If it meant her man and she would break
Under the brunt of it: she had talked it through
    with him
A hundred times . . . Let her eyeballs split, her
    head swim—
The window must have its curtain!

                                        JOSEPH AUSLANDER

*Sometimes we come close to heartbreak when it
seems that nothing but our own determination is
keeping the home above water. This is a good time
to turn away from the voice of our own weariness
and listen to gentler airs that wait to be heard.*

KINDRED

I am aware,
As I go commonly sweeping the stair,
Doing my part of the every-day care—
Human and simple my lot and my share—
I am aware of a marvelous thing:
Voices that murmur and ethers that ring
In the far stellar spaces where cherubim sing.
I am aware of the passion that pours
Down channels of fire through Infinity's doors;
Forces terrific, with melody shod,
Music that mates with the pulses of God.
I am aware of the glory that runs
From the core of myself to the core of the suns.

Bound to the stars by invisible chains,
Blaze of eternity now in my veins,
Seeing the rush of ethereal rains
Here in the midst of the every-day air—
I am aware.

I am aware,
As I sit quietly here in my chair,
Sewing or reading or braiding my hair—
Human and simple my lot and my share—
I am aware of the systems that swing
Through the aisles of creation on heavenly wing,
I am aware of a marvelous thing:
Trail of the comets in furious flight,
Thunders of beauty that shatter the night,
Terrible triumph of pageants that march
To the trumpets of time through Eternity's arch.
I am aware of the splendor that ties
All the things of the earth with the things of the
    skies,
Here in my body the heavenly heat,
Here in my flesh the melodious beat
Of the planets that circle Divinity's feet.
As I sit silently here in my chair,
I am aware.

ANGELA MORGAN

So many mothers around the globe and in such different environments, but all "bound in the bundle of life." Being mothers, we enjoy a very special kind of unity.

WOMEN WITH CHILDREN

Women with children
Have something in common,
Have something in common
That's basic and rare;
And all of their differences,
Whatever differences,
Manage in seconds
To vanish in air.

Women with children
In parks and in drugstores,
At banks, or a food market's
Vegetable stall
Will stop and will chat
In their own special language
Who otherwise never
Would bother at all.

Women with children
Belong to a union
As vast as an ocean,
As solid as stone;
One day I went shopping
And left mine behind me:
The world had a strange face
And I was alone.

MARJORIE LEE

There's a danger to it, though—this mother role.
There's a temptation to strike a pose: Mother With
Child. Sometimes there is a temptation to belittle,
ever so little, the role of the man we love, the man
we loved before this new life grew.

CAVALIERS

The strike of hoofs to greet the day,
    A snatch of song, a sense of flight:
A soldier on the king's highway
    Rides blithely to the fight.

With scarlet coat and sweeping feather,
    With steady hand and silver spur,
A gentleman rides hell-for-leather
    To win a war for her.

And we with vision incomplete
    See only this—a pale young clerk
Threading the traffic of the street
    Upon his way to work.

                        THEODOSIA GARRISON

*And if we have been selfish, if an apology is in order,
then let it be a subtle one, but dramatically staged
. . . dinner for two, perhaps, before the fire.*

APOLOGY WITHOUT WORDS

Table set with creamy linen,
    Ivory candles, silver sticks,
Crystal goblets, snowy roses . . .
    (Will he come? It's nearly six!

There's contrition, if he knew,
In this table laid for two!)

Little muffins, hot and golden,
    Crisp without and soft within;

Amber tea that tinkles coolly;
    Yellow lemon, paper-thin . . .

(Will he recognize in these
Tangible apologies?)

Jellied chicken, subtly seasoned;
    Jade-green lettuce, clean and curly;
Tiny, crimson, peeled tomatoes;
    Fresh-pulled scallions, small and pearly;

Cucumbers with edges pinked;
    Little peas as sweet as spring;
Radishes like baby tulips—
    Oh, a salad for a king!

(Can he read what salad spells,
Hear the tale a muffin tells?)

When you pass your plate tonight,
    Darling, darling, are you guessing
It's my heart I'm serving you?
    (Will you have French or Russian dressing?)

                                    LOUISE OWEN

This man in our life deserves all the building up we can give him, for he has problems too.

WHAT IS A FATHER?

A father is a thing that is forced to endure childbirth without anesthetic. A father is a thing that growls when it feels good and laughs very loud when it's scared half to death. *A father never feels entirely worthy of the worship in a child's eyes. He's never quite the hero his daughter thinks . . . never quite the man his son believes him to be . . . and this worries him, sometimes,* so he works too hard to try and smooth the rough places in the road of those of his own who will follow him.

A father is a thing that goes to war sometimes . . . and would run the other way except that war is part of his only important job in life . . . which is making the world better for his child than it has been for him.

Fathers grow old faster than people. Because they, in other wars, have to stand at the train station and wave goodbye to the uniform that climbs aboard. And while mothers cry where it shows, fathers have to stand and beam outside . . . and die inside. Fathers are what give daughters away to other men who aren't nearly good enough . . . so they can have children that are smarter than anybody's.

Fathers fight dragons almost daily. They hurry away from the breakfast table . . . off to the arena which is sometimes called an office or a workshop. There, with calloused, practiced hands they tackle the dragon with three heads: Weariness, Work, and Monotony. And they never quite win the fight but they never give up. Knights in shining armor . . . fathers in shiny trousers . . . there's little difference as they march away to each work-day.

I don't know where fathers go when they die. But I've an idea that after a good rest . . . wherever it is . . . he won't just sit on a cloud and wait for the girl he's loved and the children she bore. He'll be busy there, too . . . repairing the stairs, oiling the gates, improving the streets, smoothing the way.

AUTHOR UNKNOWN

Surely that's the kind of father Elaine V. Emans had in mind when she wrote

REVERIE

A little girl would love you, but a son
Would be so very proud to call you "Dad,"
And boast about you to his friends and run
To meet you every evening. A lad
Would go to you with all that puzzled him,
And tell you dreams of what he wished to be,
And tramp the woods and fields with you, as slim
And straight and lovely as a tender tree.

A girl would take your hand, and share your laughter
And love you deeply, but a son would mold
His speech by yours, and shape his pleasures after
Things you delight in most, and he would hold
The very fabric of his living near
To yours to make it beautiful, my dear.

ELAINE V. EMANS

There it is again! The age-old argument: which is more fun, a boy or a girl? With the question never answered yet never abandoned, no wonder these two "What Is A . . ." selections have become beloved classics.

WHAT IS A BOY?

Between the innocence of babyhood and the dignity of manhood we find a delightful creature called

16

a boy. Boys come in assorted sizes, weights, and colors, but all boys have the same creed: To enjoy every second of every minute of every hour of every day and to protest with noise (their only weapon) when their last minute is finished and the adult males pack them off to bed at night.

Boys are found everywhere—on top of, underneath, inside of, climbing on, swinging from, running around, or jumping to. Mothers love them, little girls hate them, older sisters and brothers tolerate them, adults ignore them, and Heaven protects them. A boy is Truth with dirt on its face, Beauty with a cut on its finger, Wisdom with bubble gum in its hair, and the Hope of the future with a frog in its pocket.

When you are busy, a boy is an inconsiderate, bothersome, intruding jangle of noise. When you want him to make a good impression, his brain turns to jelly or else he becomes a savage, sadistic, jungle creature bent on destroying the world and himself with it.

A boy is a composite—he has the appetite of a horse, the digestion of a sword swallower, the energy of a pocket-size atomic bomb, the curiosity of a cat, the lungs of a dictator, the imagination of a Paul Bunyan, the shyness of a violet, the audacity of a steel trap, the enthusiasm of a firecracker, and when he makes something he has five thumbs on each hand.

He likes ice cream, knives, saws, Christmas, comic books, the boy across the street, woods, water (in its natural habitat), large animals, Dad, trains, Saturday mornings, and fire engines. He is not much for Sunday School, company, schools, books without pictures, music lessons, neckties, barbers, girls, overcoats, adults, or bedtime.

17

Nobody else is so early to rise, or so late to supper. Nobody else gets so much fun out of trees, dogs, and breezes. Nobody else can cram into one pocket a rusty knife, a half-eaten apple, three feet of string, an empty Bull Durham sack, two gum drops, six cents, a slingshot, a chunk of unknown substance, and a genuine supersonic code ring with a secret compartment.

A boy is a magical creature—you can lock him out of your work shop, but you can't lock him out of your heart. You can get him out of your study, but you can't get him out of your mind. Might as well give up—he is your captor, your jailer, your boss, and your master—a freckled-face, pint-sized, cat-chasing, bundle of noise. But when you come home at night with only the shattered pieces of your hopes and dreams, he can mend them like new with the two magic words—"Hi Dad!"

ALAN BECK

WHAT IS A GIRL?

Little Girls are the nicest things that happen to people. They are born with a little bit of angel-shine about them and though it wears thin sometimes, there is always enough left to lasso your heart —even when they are sitting in the mud, or crying temperamental tears, or parading up the street in mother's best clothes.

A little girl can be sweeter (and badder) oftener than anyone else in the world. She can jitter around, and stomp, and make funny noises that frazzle your nerves, yet just when you open your mouth, she stands there demure with that special look in her eyes. A girl is Innocence playing in the mud, Beauty standing on its head, and Motherhood dragging a doll by the foot.

Girls are available in five colors—black, white, red, yellow, or brown, yet Mother Nature always manages to select your favorite color when you place your order. They disprove the law of supply and demand—there are millions of little girls, but each is as precious as rubies.

God borrows from many creatures to make a little girl. He uses the song of a bird, the squeal of a pig, the stubbornness of a mule, the antics of a monkey, the spryness of a grasshopper, the slyness of a fox, the softness of a kitten, and to top it all off He adds the mysterious mind of a woman.

A little girl likes new shoes, party dresses, small animals, first grade, noise makers, the girl next door, dolls, make-believe, dancing lessons, ice cream, kitchens, coloring books, make-up, cans of water, going visiting, tea parties, and one boy. She doesn't care so much for visitors, boys in general, large dogs, hand-me-downs, straight chairs, vegetables, snow suits, or staying in the front yard. She is loudest when you are thinking, the prettiest when she has provoked you, the busiest at bedtime, the quietest when you want to show her off, and the most flirtatious when she absolutely must not get the best of you again.

Who else can cause you more grief, joy, irritation, satisfaction, embarrassment, and genuine delight than this combination of Eve, Salome, and Florence Nightingale? She can muss up your home, your hair, and your dignity—spend your money, your time, and your temper—then just when your patience is ready to crack, her sunshine peeks through and you've lost again.

Yes, she is a nerve-racking nuisance, just a noisy bundle of mischief. But when your dreams tumble down and the world is a mess—when it seems you are pretty much of a fool after all—she can make you a king when she climbs on your knee and whispers, "I love you best of all!"

ALAN BECK

Mr. Beck has a perceptive portrait of a mother, too.

Little Girls, it is said, are made of sugar and spice and everything nice. By the time all the sugar and spice has worn off, they become mothers and all they have left is everything nice, but that lasts forever.

Still they are all different. Some mothers are chubby while others are little wisps, thin as an April breeze. Some are freckled and husky. Some are loud and others are mousy. Some are Esquimaux, Democrats, secretaries, D.A.R.s, factory workers, Sioux, socialites, and Red Cross Ladies, but mostly they are just mothers with husbands to clean up after, children to love and to spank, and houses to turn into homes.

Mothers are the people who sweep out the mountain cabins, run the carpet sweepers in Centerville, plug in the vacuum cleaners in Cedar Rapids, and see that the maids tidy up the apartments on Fifth Avenue. Mothers cook, clean, wash, mend, dream, punish, wheedle, improvise, cajole, and make things go twice as far as a man ever could. Children are what they read to, listen for, play with, watch over, think about, pray for, worry with, do without because of, and brag to the neighbors about. A bobby pin and gummed tape are Mother's kit of tools; intuition is her college degree; and a new hat is her Declaration of Independence.

All mothers, from the Arctic Circle to the Equator, have the reputation of being wonderful cooks. The older we become and the farther we wander, the more we are convinced that nobody anywhere can make quite as good an apple pie (or jerked walrus goulash) as Mother. Dear old Mother—was she really the cook we thought her to be back in the days when our cast-iron stomachs could digest anything we could chew up?

Mothers are patient souls. Your Mother, in particular, must have been a blue ribbon patience winner when you were young. How else could she have raised such a one as you? Patience alone couldn't have done it; it took many cubic miles of love and lucky for you (lucky for all of us) that a mother's heart is as boundless as the universe itself. Anyone else would have scrubbed our ears, dressed us in our Sunday best, and sent us packing to the nearest orphans home after the first two or three years of trying to convert a small savage into a civilized boy or girl.

When we were little, Mother was everything to us—the police department, the board of education, the department of public works, the recreation commission, the finance department, the court of correction. She was a busy person. The only reason she wasn't driven out of her mind is because she was a mother with the leadership of Moses, the courage of Daniel, and the patience of Job.

All mothers are beautiful when they are young—remember? Then as the years turn into decades, Mother meets another man besides Dad and this man is Old Father Time. Her fresh beauty changes after she and Old Father Time get to be good friends. There are little cut lines on her thumb made by the paring knife and the winter winds roughen her cheeks when she hangs out the clothes (even when she uses all those magic creams). She doesn't carry the grocery bags so jauntily as when you were skipping along by her side. And her eyes, once dancing, are tired because they have seen so many, many things. Then one day, Mother looks in the mirror and says to herself, "I am no longer pretty," and it is a sad and lonely day. Mother is seldom wrong, but she was wrong that time. The beauty of mothers is as indestructible as Faith, Hope, and Love because mothers are all these things and more.

When the years roll on and the children scatter to the faraway places of the earth, Mother's job is done. Her little ones have become young men and women, for better or for worse, and there is nothing left that she possibly can do. Now she can sit back and relax and take things easy in the golden autumn of her life. But does she? No! Now she has grandchildren to visit, to plan for, to buy for, to make for, to sew for, to knit for, and if she lives long enough she becomes a great-grandmother. Only then can she stop and rest and spend the remainder of her days just being as beautiful as only great-grandmothers can be.

But whether she be eighteen or eighty, Mother is an irreplaceable treasure. None other will ever love you half so well or half so foolishly. None other will be so sure you are right, good and worthy. Of course, sometimes she is wrong, but God love her for it and keep her forever in His grace.

ALAN BECK

That applies to all mothers, you know. Stepmothers, for instance, those self-less women who move into the heart and home of a lonely child and bring love and laughter back again to stay. Did you know that it was of his stepmother that Lincoln said: "All that I am or hope to be, I owe to my angel Mother"? Surely there are no more dedicated women anywhere than those blessed women who are not mothers in any official sense, but have simply "taken a child to raise" . . .

She was old and yet she was ageless—in the manner of such staunch country widows. Gaunt, plain-spoken, and hard of arm, she could stand up to three of the toughest, shrewdest cattle dealers in Pleasants County and get every penny she thought her hog was worth. Or if pork was off that year she would butcher and can her own sausage and smoke her own hams and have enough left over to present the preacher's family with a nice meal of spareribs. In the summer she sent the children into the woodlands and brush filth with buckets for berries, and it was her old, wise hands that taught their young fingers how to pick them and schooled their eyes in the ways of berry-finding. She had a cow and she churned her own butter and sold it at New Economy wrapped in cool, damp swaths of immaculate muslin. She had chickens and their eggs went to market, too, in a bright yellow basket spread across with a napkin. From the fat of her butchered hog she made soap, standing in a drenching March rain beside her brawling iron kettle in the back yard till the task was done. Fifteen miles down river at Parkersburg a waitress had short-changed her and that was a quarter of a century before and she had never gone to that town again.

Widowed a full forty years before, she had raised a son and seen him off into the world but she had soon grown lonely in the haunted stillnesses of the old home and so there had never been a time in the quarter of a century since that her house had not sheltered a child. And children were easy to come by in the river lands. Many a dark-haired farm girl lost her wits to an August moon and the mouth of a cunning lover and found herself, after he had gone away to work in Pittsburgh or Detroit, with the fruit of their ecstasy squalling and unwelcome in her poor mother's kitchen. Once the child was weaned and toddling it was to Rachel Cooper's door that he was carried, like as not, and there was never the bad word uttered for what he was: poor little woods' colt. On Sundays his mother might come for a visit and a walk with him in the fields and at sundown he would be returned to Rachel's bed and board, unprotesting. She fed her children till they were rosy and full, scrubbed them till they were red and squalling, spanked them when there was cause, and taught them the Lord's tales on Sabbath mornings. . . .

And this was the house of Rachel Cooper—a strong tree with branches for many birds. And so the coming of two more did not make much of a difference. They were children and they were hungry and they needed love and a bath and a spanking and sometimes Rachel would think when she looked at them, any of them: 'Deed to God, sometimes I feel like I'm playin' a big joke on the Lord. Why, when He comes looking for old folks He won't even see me—He'll see them kids and maybe He'll just pass on by and say: Why, shoot! That there's a *mother!* I can't take her!

DAVIS GRUBB

So many mothers, from so many spheres, yet all one so that at last it has become a timeless, universal symbol—mother and infant, Madonna and Child.

THE MAID-SERVANT AT THE INN

"It's queer," she said; "I see the light
    As plain as I beheld it then,
All silver-like and calm and bright—
    We've not had stars like that again!

"And she was such a gentle thing
    To birth a baby in the cold.
The barn was dark and frightening—
    This new one's better than the old.

"I mind my eyes were full of tears,
    For I was young, and quick distressed,

But she was less than me in years
    That held a son against her breast.

"I never saw a sweeter child—
    The little one, the darling one!—
I mind I told her, when he smiled
    You'd know he was his mother's son.

"It's queer that I should see them so—
    The time they came to Bethlehem
Was more than thirty years ago;
    I've prayed that all is well with them."

DOROTHY PARKER

Sunny Days

Quite suddenly, between one bright morning and the next, your baby isn't a baby any more. He's walking now, and that makes all the difference.

PAGE FOR A DIARY

The world did not notice,
None later could say
The hour, the moment,
The gold-rimmed day;
For some small things
That now and then
We wonder how
And wonder when
Are often lost
From the spool of Time,
As a scrap of thread
Or a line of rhyme.

The grass did not notice,
Each soft green blade
Denied the wonder
His small foot made
In its new white shoe,
How his eyes grew wide
With sky and cloud
And earth and pride!
So I set him here
In a song's gold key
Beyond the rust
Of memory,
In his new blue suit,
With his soft hair curled,
This gay first time
He stepped on the world.

GLADYS MCKEE

He is talking now, too. And that makes even more difference! Once the children are talking, life is never dull!

A startled Memphis mother heard her small son urge his brother: "Here, Johnny, try this candy. It tastes just like a grasshopper."

LYDEL SIMS

And after they are talking many a pearl of wisdom drops from very young lips:

Little girls' bottoms are really a wonderful gift from heaven for calming the nerves of mothers. I know perfectly well that's what they were invented for, for hands have hollows and bottoms have humps.

MINOU DROUET

Now begin the days when you see differences developing, the gradual shaping toward the person she will someday be.

THE LITTLE DARK ONE

Steve is Davy Crockett—
His cap of cobweb coonskin—
And Johnny is a Ranger
On a nonexistent roan—

So round and round the garden
Where Captain Hook and Tinker
And Hopalong and Robber Joe
And all their sort are known.

But Catharine—but Catharine
Walks softly through the roses,
Her baby doll in crook of arm—
She rides no role nor horse.

"And who are *you*, with roses crowned?"
She answers with her grave eyes round:
"I'm Catharine—just Catharine,
I'm Catharine, of course."

So round and round the garden
They travel in the shadows
Of things that seem and things that are
(Like people who are grown)
But Catharine, just Catharine
Already knows the mystery
And magic and enough-to-be
Of Catharine alone!

ELIZABETH HENLEY

A child begins to walk with sureness through his world, these sunny golden days, secure because he knows his own role in that world.

THE FOUR-YEAR-OLD "MORNING CHILD"

This is the story of a morning child.

He wakes up singing in the morning, for morning is his most special time. He goes to school in the morning, to a school for four-year-old people. Being a morning child is no trifling matter; it is his identification; his link with a larger life.

His acceptance of himself as the lowest man on the grade-school totem pole is perfect. He is glad to be in the school at all. His satisfaction with his role in the family is complete. He is "de littles' boy," but he also will grow up to be just like Daddy.

He has found new friends at school. He knows a little girl named Karen, and he says she is "a cutie pie." He knows a little girl named Sally; she asked him to marry her, but he told her that he didn't think he had to get married if he didn't want to. He knows a boy named Tommy, and together they are the toughest fighters and the best builders with blocks in the class.

He knows a kindergarten teacher whose experience, talent and warmth make him feel loved, and who makes every step in learning a happy one.

This is our morning child. He has more gaiety, more songs, more dances, more talk, more lost mittens, more serious business, more expectation of everything, more social security than any adult.

May it always be morning!

KATY COLLINS, from *Spousekeeping*

He is feeling his way into his role in the family, too. Reaching out for his place in the circle of family love.

HOME FIRE

Ofttimes across the room you come
To press a kiss against my hair,
To hold me for no cause at all,
Save love. At once our small ones there
Come laughing, make a ring-around.
So does devotion strike a spark
That showers into golden light,
Gathering children in its arc.

VIRGINIA MOODY HAGAN

Some of this searching and reaching is accomplished by maddening, incessant, questioning chatter. Some-

times mothers, too, learn from the chatter and the questions. . . .

TAFFY AND ME

Taffy helps me hang the clothes. She hands me the clothespins. She hands them to me fast when I'm hanging the sheets, and she hands them to me slowly when I'm hanging the socks.

"I got that for my birthday," says Taffy, pointing to her sunsuit, "when I was this many." She holds up two fingers. "Do you remember when I was a little girl?"

"Yes. Quite well."

"So do I. Remember when I was this many fingers and liked onions?"

"Yes."

"I still do."

"You still like onions?"

"No. I still remember when I was this many fingers and liked onions. But I don't any more."

"You don't like onions any more."

"I already said that."

"I know. I just thought—"

"I saw the man in the moon last night," says Taffy, turning her face to the sky.

"Did you?"

"Yes. He was wearing a swimming hat, and he was riding a bicycle real fast with wheels on it."

"Why?"

"To keep his hair from not getting wet," she explains.

"Oh, of course. I should have known."

"See that butterfly?" she squeals.

"He looks just like my color of hair!"

She drops her clothespins. "Can he eat lunch at my house?"

Taffy doesn't wait for my answer.

She runs to catch the butterfly just the color of her hair.

MICHELLE RUTHERFORD

It's a herculean task—this finding out who they are and where they belong. To do it right, they need long hours of solitude, long hours doing nothing at all. . . .

LATE FOR CHORES

It would not be easy to explain
Why he was late. He blamed the rain
That came when the last load of the hay
Turned to the barn—and a shorter way
Across the field seemed meant for him.
He reached the willows, cool and dim
Beside the pasture brook. In his wake
His dog came barking, and stopped to shake
The shining drops with joy, and then
Across the brook they found again
The cave the boy had dug, last year,
Deep in the high bank. It was clear
Of fallen clay, and the place was dry,
And the silver rain came slanting by
The door, and above, the willows swayed,
And below, the brook new music played.

The little fire he lighted there
Made sweet smoke on the musky air,
And the dog curled up at last and sighed
And went to sleep. The boy had tried
To keep awake; but the next he knew
The dusk crept in, and the rain was through.
He was late for chores; but so were the men
Unloading the hay, and he wondered then
If his father had dozed a while—like the son—
With the rain on the roof, and the haying done.

GLENN WARD DRESBACH

*Even as he is growing away from you in some ways,
home is still the center of his being. Knowing that
the right kind of home is the balance wheel of a
child's universe, what parent has not felt the need to
ask for help in creating such a home?*

PRAYER FOR A NEW HOUSE

Dear Lord, before we enter in,
Go Thou before us, opening the door.
First give Thy blessing, ere the good friends come
To bless it. First Thy feet upon the floor,
Treading the untried carpet. Fill each room
With peace and loving-kindness. Make the air
Congenial, that no swift or careless word
Shall sound among these walls, and everywhere
Spread gentleness—beside the waiting hearth,
The kitchen, parlor, in the nursery,
And in the guestroom. Keep the windows clean
That face the dawn and sunset, that we see

Always the splendor of the world outside;
Also, that strangers, neighbors passing by
Shall sense a lovely world of peace inside.
Keep bright the torch lamps at the door when sky
And wind are menacing. Make the door
So strong that storm and fear shall not intrude,
So easy opened that a child's soft hand
Can swing it wide. Yet one thing more we pray—
Grant we shall love home always—as today.

PHILIP JEROME CLEVELAND

That "lovely world of peace inside" sometimes seems, in such tense times, a mirage, a Utopian delusion. For every parent there come times when we cry out, "Where can we find peace today?"

The instinct is to toss aside the daily paper in total discouragement. There seems to be no peace, anywhere, only dissension, misery, violence, and misunderstanding. Everywhere the story is the same: man's inability to live with man in harmony.

The war was supposed to have ended nearly three years ago. But these years of so-called peace have been festering with dreadful infections, and the world is running a high fever in prelude to danger.

Turn from the headlines and the temper is not much better. There is murder on the radio, murder on the screen, murder on the printed page, and murder on the next block. Although we in America are not stalked by hunger and cold, food and shelter and clothing have not brought peace to the spirits of the richest people in the world.

So where can we find the peace we crave and are denied? In our own homes, perhaps. On our own acres, if we have any. But most of all, in our hearts. There is the only inviolable refuge.

But how find it there? How build up an oasis of calm that can withstand the frightful outer pressures of evil?

The answer is to thrust away the nagging small immediacies and dig into the changeless matter of creation. If you can do this, you come upon a pattern which is itself assurance that the basis of life is not chaos but order, not dissonance but harmony. The majestic march of planets and of seasons, the slow, magnetic ebb and pulse of tides, the cadences of genius, the cold, long preparation of earth for its renewal each spring—these are all evidences of this order, all denials of chaos. But you need not look that far. Peace is in the warm word of a neighbor; in the innumerable daily acts of human decency that form a barrier to chaos. Chaos is man-made, and by that token can be man-dispelled.

We can not look for peace. We must make it in ourselves.

From *Vogue*

In the search for peace, our role of mother assumes an awesome responsibility, for whether or not we wish it, we set the tone, the mood of the home. But even if we attain the pinnacle of order and peace within our walls, we know full well that home is not enough. There is a world outside, a world of laughter and long lazy days for exploring and all the shining discoveries outside the walls of home.

EVERY CHILD

Every child should know a hill,
And the clean joy of running down its long slope
With the wind in his hair.
He should know a tree—
The comfort of its cool lap of shade,
And the supple strength of its arms
Balancing him between earth and sky
So he is the creature of both.
He should know bits of singing water—
The strange mysteries of its depths,
And the long sweet grasses that border it.

Every child should know some scrap
Of uninterrupted sky, to shout against;
And have one star, dependable and bright,
For wishing on.

EDNA CASLER JOLL

*Every child needs, too, to know solemn moments of
wonder, moments of clear, stabbing awareness of
what a beautiful world this is.*

One of life's major tragedies, both for parents and
for children, lies in the fact that the joys of today
are all about us, unrecognized. Obviously, a father
would defeat his purpose (and be a bore) if he
studded the family conversation with rhapsodic
exclamations, "What a good time I'm having shining my shoes! The rhythm of the brush! The red-
olence of the shoe cream! The highlights that the

sunshine makes upon the polished leather!" Likewise a mother would kill the thing she tries to foster if she went about exclaiming, "Ah me! the silver egg-beater in a yellow bowl whipping thick white cream! What color! What texture! What beauty!" And yet it is just such unexpected homely incidents which make the sensitive individual catch his breath with wonder for the manifold beauties of everyday life; sunshine edging the drawn window shade and falling slantwise across a dark rug; a child bouncing upstairs with her own joyous rhythm; dandelions rioting in a vacant lot; rusty grasses along the roadside—these and a thousand other wonders crowding the most commonplace day.

Awareness, or learning to live as one goes, is distinctly a habit. A parent may have to cultivate the habit in himself before he can cultivate it in his children. But once awareness becomes a habit, then the spirit rushes forth with ecstasy to moments of aliveness it would otherwise have missed—and never know how great was its poverty in the missing.

MARGUERITTE HARMON BRO

But most of all they need (oh, how desperately they need it!) someone who understands. I have long thought that William Toland is a very lucky little boy.

WILLIAM MAKES GOOD

"I know I have been bad," says William. "You can punish me."

My heart sinks. "What have you done?"

"Well," says William, firmly clasping his muddy hands, and speaking slowly so I will understand, "I took daddy's flower, and I pulled it up out of its pot."

"Whatever for, William?"

"To see what makes it grow."

"Oh." (What else is there to say?)

"I found its strings down in the ground, and a great big worm too. And now I know, I won't ever have to pull it up again." He puts out his hand. "But you can spank me for this time."

I take his muddy fist in mine, and hand in hand we go into the kitchen for our lunch. (William is so wonderfully sure of what is Wrong, and what is Right. I wish I knew. I wish I could ask his advice.)

POLLY TOLAND

Fortunately, this love they crave, this love they need, is something mothers possess in full supply. Everything a mother does from dawn to dark bespeaks the love she has for her brood. This "Song For a Husband" might just as aptly be entitled "Song For a Family". . . .

SONG FOR A HUSBAND

Out in the sun a little wind is singing
   Lyrics to the leaves and sighing grass.
Where is the song of love I should be bringing?
   Am I some lesser thing than winds that pass?
And yet when evening takes its inventory

By firelight, it can count my poems, too:
The crisp shirts, and the spicy golden glory
   Of pumpkin pies, the savory scent of stew.
What words that wind or I could ever write
   Would be as sweet as smooth sheets on a bed?
Where are lovers' lyrics half so bright
   To hungry hearts as the warmth of fresh-baked
      bread?
And so I write my songs in a homely hand,
   But in a language love can understand.

PATRICIA M. JORDAN

The creation of a fine family feeling depends not only on love, but on doing things together as a family unit. Most of us find—to our sorrow—that it is on Mother's shoulders that the weight of these arrangements most often falls. Take the matter of playing games together, for instance—if you feel you're durable enough.

Most parents realize the importance of healthy, happy, wholesome family fun, in which all the family take part. This helps to give the children a sense of *belonging*. I don't know what it gives the parents.

A great many parents would *like* to spend time with their children and play with them, but actually don't know how. Really, there are many games for the whole family, in which every member can participate, even the smallest. As the sizes of families range from very small to utter madness, all my suggestions for games are carefully planned to be suitable for any number and for any ages.

A rainy Saturday or Sunday afternoon is the best possible time for family fun, and here is a game you will all enjoy. It requires no equipment other than pencils, paper, and a phonograph. Each member of the family sits on the floor, forming a circle. They then count off by twos, thus forming two teams. Just to make it more exciting, give the teams names, like Tigers and the Bears, or the Lilies and the Azaleas. One of the children (and this is an excellent job for the littlest) may hand round paper and pencils. Another child then starts a record on the phonograph. Any good record will do, though Duke Ellington is a better choice. The parents have previously hidden in their pockets thirty-five cents per child. When the music starts each player writes as fast as he can all the rivers of South America beginning with the letter Y. Allow about ninety seconds for this. Then the child tending the phonograph turns it off, and collects the papers and pencils, the parents distribute the thirty-five cents to each child and the parents choose to see which one drives the children down to the movie house for the kiddie matinee complete with chaperon. They're showing *The Monster From the Moon* and *The Horror From Outer Space*, which should be a *good* double bill.

Another simple little game that the whole family will enjoy is one that we play often, as it requires no special equipment. In this game, the father offers a prize to the child who can maintain absolute silence for the longest period of time, and the prize increases with the length of time the game lasts.

Some children become quite adept at this game, learning after some practice to keep silent for as much as ten or twelve minutes at a time. This game is not only *grand fun* for everyone, but is truly educational as well, for if the prizes awarded to the winners are halfway decent, the children learn from practical experience that SILENCE IS TRULY GOLDEN. Sometimes caramels or jawbreakers judiciously offered just before the game starts can help to prolong the fun.

Another jolly little game that we all enjoy is called "hide." This is similar to "hide and seek," but in "hide" the children all run and find good hiding places. While they are hiding, the parents settle down comfortably in the living room and read the Sunday papers. This is a game that is full of merriment for all, as well as being wholesome and beneficial to the parents.

ELINOR GOULDING SMITH

But there are magic moments, too, moments of almost unbearable tenderness and closeness. The moment will pass, but the emotion it engendered is often remembered for long, long years.

PERFECT MOMENT

Somewhere along the road between "beginning" and "ending" there is a perfect moment for every living soul. There may possibly be more than one. But for the most part we are too busy, too young, too adult, too sophisticated, too this or too that to recognize it—and so the moment may be lost.

My perfect moment came when I was eight years old. I awoke one spring night to find moonlight flooding my room through the open window. It was so bright that I sat up in bed. There was no sound at all anywhere. The air was soft and heavy with the fragrance of pear blossoms and honeysuckle.

I crept out of bed and tiptoed softly out of the house. Eight-year-olds were not supposed to be astir at this hour. But I wanted to sit in the swing for a while and watch the moonlight. As I closed the door behind me, I saw my mother sitting on the porch steps. She looked up and smiled and, putting her finger to her lips, reached out with her other hand and drew me down beside her. I sat as close as I could and she put her arm around me.

The whole countryside was hushed and sleeping; no lights burned in any house. The moonlight was liquid silver and so bright we could see the dark outline of the woods a mile away. "Isn't it beautiful?" I whispered, and Mother's arm tightened about me.

Our shepherd dog, Frollo, came across the lawn and stretched himself out contentedly, his head on Mother's lap. For a long time we were all three perfectly still. The stars were pale and far away. Now and then the moonlight would strike a leaf of the Marechal Niel rose beside the porch and be caught for an instant in a dewdrop like a tiny living spark. The shrubs were hung with necklaces of diamonds, and the grass was sweet with dampness.

We knew that in the dark woods there were movement and sound among the wild things—the rabbits and squirrels, the oppossums and chipmunks, as they moved about in their own world. And in the

45

shadowy garden, and in the fields, things were grow-ing. In the meadow the foal slept beside its mother, and nearby a young calf nuzzled its mother.

Very soon the blossoms on the fruit trees would loose their petals in a pink-and-white snowfall, and in their place the young fruit would appear. The wild-plum thicket would be filled with plums, round and glowing like tiny lanterns, made sweet by the sun and cool by the rain. In another field the young corn plants were inching their way upward. Melons would soon dot the trailing vines where now the squash-like blooms were replenishing their nectar in preparation for the onrush of bees in the morning.

In all this great brooding silence that seemed so infinite, the miracle of life was going on unseen and unheard. The bird sitting on her eggs in the mulberry tree carried out a divine purpose. The hills, undisturbed by passing centuries, proclaimed strength and grandeur. The moving of the stars, the planets, the countless worlds, all were governed and held within the safety of the omnipotent yet gentle hand of the Creator.

Mother pointed toward the cedar tree. "Look," she whispered softly, "that star seems caught in the branches."

As we watched it, suddenly from the topmost point of a pear tree a mockingbird burst into song. It was as though the joy that overflowed his heart must find expression. The notes were pure gold, free and clear and liquid as the moonlight, rising, falling, meltingly sweet. At times they were so soft as to be barely audible; then he would sing out, a rapturous profondo. As suddenly as it had begun, the concert ended and the night was silvery still again.

An eight-year-old does not analyze his thoughts,

he may not even be aware that he is surrounded by infinity. But he sees a star impaled on the branch of a cedar tree, and knows pure ecstasy. He hears a mockingbird sing in the moonlight, and is filled with speechless joy. He feels his mother's arms about him, and knows complete security.

GLADYS BELL

We who are parents are the architects of memory—and that is as proud a vocation as any that I know.

ARDIS WHITMAN

Some of these memories we may never know about; they may be locked away in the very special part of his heart a child keeps just for memories, where they may hearten and sustain him for three-quarters of a century of living. . . .

THE SECRET HEART

Across the years he could recall
His father one way best of all.

In the stillest hour of night
The boy awakened to a light.

Half in dreams, he saw his sire
With his great hands full of fire.

The man had struck a match to see
If his son slept peacefully.

He held his palms each side the spark
His love had kindled in the dark.

His two hands were curved apart
In the semblance of a heart.

He wore, it seemed to his small son,
A bare heart on his hidden one,

A heart that gave out such a glow
No son awake could bear to know.

It showed a look upon a face
Too tender for the day to trace.

One instant, it lit all about,
And then the secret heart went out.

But it shone long enough for one
To know that hands held up the sun.

ROBERT P. TRISTRAM COFFIN

The snapshots we paste in a leather-bound album (or, more likely, stuff into the top drawer of the hall table!) are priceless, but even more precious are those scenes we carry in our memories, scenes from the sunny days when the children were very small: a dark-eyed toddler in blue sleepers, drinking milk from a pewter cup . . . your smallest daughter, the Easter she wore the yellow coat . . . a freckle-faced little boy, proudly holding high a fistful of long-stemmed dandelions. . . .

CORSAGE

Mother, Mother,
The florist's boy knocks,
With his hat in his hand
And a great green box.

Hurry, lift the cover;
See, untie the bow . . .
Four pink camellias
Fastened in a row.

Mother, mother,
Please, and shut your eyes!
This is from me.
This is a *surprise.*

Yellow dandelions
With tangly silk hair. . . .
Mother, mother,
Which shall you wear?

ETHEL JACOBSON

These mental snapshots may capture a memory as closely personal as the acquisition of your child's first dog.

DEFEAT

I know the puppy's very new,
And I know that he's lonely too—
But puppy's place is in the shed,
And not with you, deep down in bed.

Tears will not move me—not at all,
Not even though he's soft and small,
And knows you when you come from play;
The shed's his place, and there he'll stay, because—
Yes, he has lovely soft big paws,
And yes, I love his ears that flop. . . .
Now, mind: not underneath! On *top*.

BARBARA A. JONES

At first glance your favorite memory picture might appear to be a group shot, but however crowded the picture may be, a mother's eye seeks out one face.

NATIVITY SCENE—SCHOOL HALL

There will be a tinsel Star
Above a straw-filled Manger;
There will good St. Joseph stand,
Firm against all danger;
Mary, blue-gowned, sweet, will hold
The little Infant Jesus;
Angels, rosy cheeked and small,
Will sing their songs to please us.
You will look on smilingly,
Nodding side to side;
I shall need a kerchief
To catch a tear of pride;
And the miracle of Christmas
Will be for us each minute
The little donkey stands serene,
With Jimmy in it.

GLADYS MCKEE

Yet strangely, when the years have sorted out our memories, it is not these unique and dramatic days that remain most vivid, but the simple, shining details of every day.

INGREDIENTS FOR JAM

Sufficient glasses
And a good-sized kettle,
Fresh-hulled berries,
Well shaped and crimson red.
Sugar . . . and to put you
On your mettle
A small boy waiting
With a piece of bread.

MARY COOPER

But not all the memories will be of sunny days. A shadow falls across that moment when your first-born starts off to school; whether her child is brave or tearful, was there ever a mother who didn't weep, at least a little, on the first day of school?

WEE HUGHIE

He's gone to school, wee Hughie,
An' him not four,
Sure I saw the fright was in him
When he left the door,
But he took a hand o' Danny,
An' a hand o' Dan

Wi' Joe's old coat upon him—
Och, the poor wee man.
He cut the quarest figure
More stout nor thin;
An' trottin' right and steady
Wi' his toes turned in.
I watched him to the corner
O' the big turf stack.
An' the more his feet went forrit
Still his head turned back.
He was lookin' would I call him—
Och, my heart was woe—
Sure it's lost I am without him
But he be to go.
I followed to the turnin'
When they passed it by,
God help him he was cryin'
An', maybe, so was I.

ELIZABETH SHANE

Hectic Days

TO THE FIRST-GRADE TEACHER

To your clean hands I now commend
This child with lipstick kiss on ear—
And hope you find him such a friend
As I, who kept him awfully near.

He knows so little—teddy bears,
And white-railed bed, and cooky jars,
And yet is wondering about
The rest—including seas and stars.

And now it comes—the words, the books,
And what "goes into," adds, and "borrows"—
I will take care of his todays—
You, his tomorrows.

ELIZABETH HENLEY

It's so starkly final, that symbolic act of starting school. Suddenly he is not any longer ours. But was he ever ours?

55

And a woman who held a babe against her bosom said, Speak to us of Children.

And he said:

Your children are not your children.

They are the sons and daughters of Life's longing for itself.

They come through you but not from you,

And though they are with you yet they belong not to you.

You may give them your love but not your thoughts,

For they have their own thoughts.

You may house their bodies but not their souls,

For their souls dwell in the house of tomorrow, which you cannot visit, not even in your dreams.

You may strive to be like them, but seek not to make them like you.

For life goes not backward nor tarries with yesterday.

You are the bows from which your children as living arrows are sent forth.

The archer sees the mark upon the path of the infinite, and He bends you with His might that His arrows may go swift and far.

Let your bending in the Archer's hand be for gladness;

For even as He loves the arrow that flies, so He loves also the bow that is stable.

KAHLIL GIBRAN

However often we nod our heads in sage agreement, still, the day we have to face up to that fact is a shattering day for most of us. And then we face a dilemma: to fight (in vain, of course) or to learn the wisdom of "holding fast with open hands."

But never think for a moment that their need of us has passed; listen as they come pounding up the stairs after school, calling "MO—THER, WHERE ARE YOU? I'M HOME!" Then we know that home is still the center of their world.

AFTER SCHOOL

A house should have a cookie jar,
For when it's half-past three,
And children hurry home from school
As hungry as can be,
There's nothing quite so splendid
In filling children up,
As spicy, fluffy ginger cakes,
And sweet milk in a cup.

A house should have a mother
Waiting with a hug,
No matter what a boy brings home,
A puppy or a bug.
For children only loiter
When the bell rings to dismiss,
If no one's home to greet them
With a cookie or a kiss!

HELEN WELSHIMER

Life becomes more complex each day, once our children start to school. New names crop up in their

conversations—names and people strange to us—
and sometimes that creates a little hurt. New friends
—new enemies, too—new fears, new challenges. We
tell ourselves their paths cannot be rose-strewn always, but unreasonably or not, we wish it so. That's
how mothers are and have always been.

BE CAREFUL, LIFE

When she comes home from school
   Her eyes' wide blue
Will widen rounder yet;
   For here—like new—
Her broken toys will stand:
   Her teacup knows
Its handle once again;
   Her doll's head grows
In orthodox position;
   And this plate
Is whole again which met,
   Last night, its fate.

O life, hold tight my child.
   Let no quick start
Exceed your watchfulness—
   Break not her heart!

VIRGINIA SCOTT MINER

But if we cannot alter the world, how then can we
equip our children to come to terms with the world
as it is? In addition to tenderness, we can try to
teach them strength. . . . in addition to compas-
sion, we can give them steel.

In the time of your life, live—so that in that good time there shall be no ugliness or death for yourself or for any life your life touches. Seek goodness everywhere, and when it is found, bring it out of its hiding-place and let it be free and unashamed. Place in matter and in flesh the least of the values, for these are the things that hold death and must pass away. Discover in all things that which shines and is beyond corruption. Encourage virtue in whatever heart it may have been driven into secrecy and sorrow by the shame and terror of the world. Ignore the obvious, for it is unworthy of the clear eye and the kindly heart. Be the inferior of no man, nor of any man be the superior. Remember that every man is a variation of yourself. No man's guilt is not yours, nor is any man's innocence a thing apart. Despise evil and ungodliness, but not men of ungodliness or evil. These, understand. Have no shame in being kindly and gentle, but if the time comes in the time of your life to kill, kill and have no regrets. In the time of your life, live—so that in that wondrous time you shall not add to the misery and sorrow of the world, but shall smile to the infinite delight and mystery of it.

WILLIAM SAROYAN

Admittedly strong medicine, but our children live in a world beset by desperate ills. In the end, of course, they do surprisingly well without us—sometimes to our chagrin.

59

I CAN'T FIND MY APRON STRINGS

There was a time when I would have said with all confidence that the life of my only son Rufus was an open book to me. Oh, I would have conceded that I probably didn't know every vagrant thought that passed through his flitter-brain; but I made it my business to be thoroughly familiar with the mechanics of his existence. I was acquainted with everyone with whom he was acquainted; I recognized his limitations and appreciated his abilities; at any hour of the day I could tell approximately where he was and what he was doing; and I knew that were anything troubling him, I would immediately sense it, with A Mother's Instinct. At least, that was my smug assumption.

Then one blizzardy Saturday afternoon, he asked me as a favor to drive him around his paper route. He couldn't ride his bike, he said, because the snow was too deep, and since Saturday was collection day, he'd never get done on foot. Besides that, you couldn't keep the papers dry on a day like this, and he'd catch what-not all along the line from irate customers. Since all his arguments seemed valid, I agreed to furnish transportation. I'd never had a paper route myself, but naturally being A Mother and having read a lot about boys who made their starts peddling papers, I knew all there was to know about the business. You left the paper, collected the week's tariff, and that was that. If it had been any more complicated, I was sure, my son couldn't have held down the job for the past two years. He was, after all only a child. In my innocence, I even offered to help him, in the interests of speeding up delivery.

He accepted my offer. "All right, you take the left-hand side of the street and I'll take the right. That's fourteen *Enterprises* for you, and six *Globes*, and two *Records*. The first three houses are all *Enterprises*. Stick the papers inside the storm doors, and the money will be on the porch rails. The fifth house you have to ring the bell or she'll holler. The seventh and ninth houses are *Globes*, and the eighth you have to deliver at the back door. She owes for two weeks and make her give it to you. Seventy cents, and don't let her talk you out of it."

I was lost. "Wait. The first three houses the papers go in the storm doors. Then the next you ring the bell. . . ."

"No-no," he said indulgently. "You skip one house and the *next* you ring. Wouldn't it be simpler if I did them all and you kept the route book?" I allowed meekly that it would, at that. Keeping the route book consisted of checking off payments in squares provided for the purpose. I guessed I could do that.

We got along fine for about three streets. Everyone paid on schedule. At the end of the fourth street, pencil poised, I asked, "Check them all?"

"Yup, all except 39. I collect there on Mondays instead of Saturdays." I asked the reason why.

"Oh, he's always drunk on Saturdays, and half the time he doesn't understand what I want and the other half he tries to give me all his money and won't take back any change. So a couple of months ago, we had a little talk and decided it would be better if I collected on Mondays." My face must have reflected my horror. "Don't start worrying about it," my sheltered little lamb begged me. "Him and me understand each other all right. Now," he changed the subject with finality, "want to count out eleven *Enterprises* for me?"

It took me two uneventful streets to recover my composure. Then I came to a name which, as far as I could tell from my son's rather grubby bookkeeping, was about ten weeks in arrears. When he came plowing back through the drifting snow, I said, "How long are you supposed to let them go without paying? This one here . . ."

"Yeah, I know. We're supposed to drop them after a month, but the boss says to use our own judgment." What judgment of experienced dead beats can you have at twelve, I wondered. "This fellow's been having a hard time. He's been out of work for a long while, and now his wife's in the hospital. But he's just got a job, and he says he'll pay me when he gets caught up with himself."

"But what if he doesn't?"

"It comes out of my hide. But don't worry. He'll pay."

There were a lot of things I wanted to ask, like what made him so sure; and a lot of advice I wanted to give, like don't trust a sob story too far. But I kept my mouth shut, since this was my son's affair and he had to learn the ways of the world sometime, probably the hard way. For weeks I studied his face every collection day, trying to read in it any signs of disillusionment. At last I couldn't stand it any longer, so I asked.

"Who?" Rufus looked blank. "Oh, *him*. Oh, sure, he paid me up a month ago and gave me an extra buck for carrying him so long." He didn't seem even mildly elated.

How many more problems had he met and dealt with unknown to me, I wondered? How much more information did he possess about the cooking, drinking habits, and family situations of people whose names and faces meant nothing to me? It disturbed me. He was so young and inexperienced and how could I help him in a field over the wall of which I couldn't even see, let alone climb?

My son's next job was on a chicken ranch, so-called. By some persistent cross-examination, I was able to find out that the boss and his wife were all right, the work was all right, and the chickens were all right. Our family had raised a few hens when I was a child. I pictured Rufus spending his time watering and feeding the poultry, picking up the eggs, and once a week cleaning out the runs. This seemed like good wholesome work for a growing boy.

However, when he developed a stubborn cough, exhibited hands perpetually sore and abraded, and turned green at the sight of chicken fricassee, I thought perhaps I'd better investigate. My lay opinion was that without doubt the child was allergic to feathers and in that case maybe he'd better give up his egg-gathering and corn-scattering. Oh, I was full of fancy notions! The truth was much simpler, and very much removed from the pastoral idyl of my imagination.

The place of my child's employment, it turned out, had a flock of about ten thousand chickens, with a turnover of about a thousand a week. There was no picking up of eggs, since the fowl were sold as broilers before they ever got around to laying; and the feeding was done by automatic device. Rufus' work consisted of helping debeak and inoculate. All right, I never heard of those things either; but it seems that the beaks of half-grown chicks are clipped to prevent their pecking each other to death, and they are all inoculated against disease. Before either operation can take place, the individual chicken has to be caught, and that was my son's duty. All day long he caught chickens, entering a pen of two hundred, plunging into the hysterical mass, getting his hands pecked and clawed and nicked by inoculation needles, and breathing poor air in the dust raised by the frantic beating of wings. That accounted for all his symptoms, I thought, including aversion to chicken fricassee.

"It doesn't sound like a very pleasant job," I commented with restraint. Personally I thought it sounded horrible. "Why didn't you tell me?"

He shrugged. "At least it's a job, and that's more than some kids have got. It doesn't bother me much except when I go to bed and close my eyes. All I see then is hens, hens, hens flying around. That and the dead ones. Darned fools, when you try to catch them, they all pile up at the end of the pen and the bottom ones smother. When I go to eat chicken, all I can think of is those dead hens." You poor kid, I thought. With a little encouragement, I'd have burst into tears. "Say, Ma," he asked suddenly, "did you ever pick up a chicken?"

Mastering my emotion, I said that yes, I had picked up many chickens.

"Hot, ain't they?" I don't know what I'd expected, but it wasn't that. I started laughing, which was just as well.

I never did find out much about Rufus' job at the garage. In theory, he washed cars, changed tires, and pumped gas for customers. However, I came out of the chain store one day to find my son in deep consultation with a well-dressed stranger. Rufus was shaking his head and looking judicious. "She shouldn't do that," he said. "Let me take a look." The man climbed into a brand-new Lincoln parked at the curb, released the hood, and Rufus plunged elbow-deep into the innards of the motor. I prevented myself with difficulty from screaming, "Don't touch! Those things run into money!" I was in no financial position to replace Lincolns ruined by my son's feckless attention.

"Now try her," Rufus instructed with the confident aplomb of a high-priced specialist. The owner stepped on the starter, the motor purred into life, and Rufus announced, "She's okay now."

When the stranger had driven away. I told him, "You mustn't fool around with other people's cars. Who was that, anyhow? What were you doing under his hood? You might have busted something, and. . . ."

"Gee *whiz*, Ma," he expostulated, "you'd think I was born yesterday! There wasn't nothing much the matter with that Lincoln. You ought to have seen the job we had last week. Oh boy, timing off, feed line plugged, wiring shorted. . . ."

And here I'd been changing blown-out fuses myself, and sending out my repairs around the house to be fixed! Why don't kids ever *tell* you anything?

Like most boys who live in country towns, Rufus has a list of clients whose lawns he mows in summer and whose paths he shovels in winter. These are largely older women, acquaintances of mine, either unmarried or widowed, who have no male of their own to tend these chores. I'm quite accustomed to answering the phone and delivering such messages as, "Mrs. Bridges would like you to go over Saturday and bring down her porch furniture from the attic." Those transactions are routine and quite comprehensible to me. Where I get fouled up is when the phone rings and a tear-choked voice requests, "Will you tell Rufus he died last night, and will he please come over after school and bury him?"

When I repeat the tale to Rufus he just says, "Yeah? That's too bad, but here today and gone tomorrow. Well, I better get over there before she has a fit." And he hops on his bike and is off like the wind, leaving me biting my nails with frustrated curiosity. At dinner time I manage to pry loose the information that it was Miss Burton's love bird that died, after a long illness. I hadn't even known he was sick. Heck, I hadn't even known she had a love bird.

"You didn't!" Rufus exclaims, "I guess you don't know her very well, do you? She talks about it enough, or she did. Now she says she's never going to have another pet, but of course she will. They always do."

"Who always. . . . Oh, skip it. I take it that you feel that you do know Miss Burton very well."

"Well enough," he says cryptically. That ends that discussion.

Early last summer Rufus informed me that he had a job helping a dairy farmer get in his hay. He had to be at the farm at half past seven, and he wouldn't be home until dark, since with haying you work as long as the light and the weather last. That sounded reasonable to me, so I was a little surprised when after two weeks of this program, he drove a big truckload of milk cans into the yard, at nine in the morning, and asked me if I'd like to help him.

"Help you what?" I demanded. "And does Mr. Hogg know you're out in his truck? After all, you haven't had your driver's license too long. And anyhow, I thought you were haying."

He sighed deeply. "I was afraid of this. You always have to have everything *explained*." He adopted an air of elaborate patience. "In simple words, you can't start haying until the dew is off the grass, which won't be for an hour. In the meantime, someone has to take the milk to the creamery. Now, do you want to come or not?"

I could plainly see that if I intended to keep even a rough check on my off-spring's activities, I'd better go along with him. Always having to have everything *explained* came dangerously close to nagging. I went, and I learned a lot of interesting things, including the fact that a good way to get a sprained back is to lift ten-gallon cans of milk from a low truck body to a high loading platform. There were doubtless a lot of things I didn't learn, but at that point I started to give up.

I didn't completely give up, though, until last week. Rufus told me that he was going to spend his winter vacation by working at a turkey-processing plant two towns away where they killed turkeys and prepared them for market. He'd arranged for transportation: he'd meet Norm, whoever he was, at Charlie's Diner at six in the morning. All I had to worry about was putting up a lunch and seeing that the alarm clock was set for 5:30. This seemed within my limited abilities, but after ten days I forgot to set the alarm. Rufus wasn't at Charlie's, Norm went off without him, and it was up to me to see that he got to work, since I was the one who had failed with the alarm clock.

Shivering and hungry in the pitch black of a winter predawn, I drove him by obscure back roads to a long tumble-down shed in a field. Dim lights burned within, illuminating vaguely some sinister figures bundled against the cold and wearing rubber aprons. An ugly black mongrel came tearing out, slavering and snarling savagely. Good Lord, I thought, what a horrible setup! I can't leave my child here with this bunch of thugs. That dog is only waiting to rip his throat out. I'm going to take him straight home.

But before I could open my chattering teeth to say so, he'd jumped out of the car. "Hello, Bandit!" he greeted the dog affectionately, and the great beast swooned with silly joy. The men in the shed crowded to the door, laughing. "Sure as heck thought you weren't going to make it this morning, Boy!" they shouted, and all the unshaven, villainous faces were transfigured with good humor and friendliness.

"Okay, okay," said one who seemed to be in charge. "We haven't got all day. Shake the lead out of your pants, Rufus, and get an apron on. I want you to shackle today."

That's when I gave up. I didn't know what shackling was, and I didn't try to find out. Driving back home alone in the red sunrise, I faced the fact that my child had a life of his own that he was perfectly competent to handle. He's been doing it for years, during which most of my fussing and worrying had

68

been so much wasted energy. From now on, I resolved, I was going to bear in mind the truth that the young are much more resourceful, adaptable and capable than their poor mothers, who foster a delusion of indispensability, are willing to accept.

It'll be very good for both of us, if I can do it.

LOUISE DICKINSON RICH

But let's not feel too helpless; no less an authority than Philip Wylie (who has castigated American "Moms" so scathingly) has given us a talisman to restore our shattered egos after such encounters.

Be as unsentimental about it as you wish, there is still no denying that the homemaker moves in the honorable tradition of the makers and molders of society. Here you are and here is the plastic clay. And when you have done with it what you will, here after all is the pivot center of the world.

PHILIP WYLIE

There is, of course, a warning there. The molding may be for good or for ill. Who of us would say "I am wise enough to choose the mold in which I'll shape my child"? Yet sometimes we act as though we had that wisdom. When I am tempted to play God that way, I go off somewhere alone and re-read this Responsive Reading distributed at church last Children's Day:

LITANY FOR CHILDREN'S DAY

We have dedicated this day to our children;

And for our children on this day,
We dream great dreams of their tomorrows.

Let this be our dream for our children:
That they may always know,
In the brief and fleeting years of childhood,
The warmth of our unfailing love—

For only thus shall they learn to love.

Let this be our dream for our children:
That they may always, even in their youngest years
Receive our full respect as persons—

For only thus shall they gain self-respect,
And learn respect for others.

Let this be our dream for our children:
That they may always find us, their elders,
Seeking to preserve and to create things of endur-
ing beauty—

For only thus shall they learn to love the beautiful, and to live beautifully.

Let this be our dream for our children:
That they may ever find us, their elders,
Open and receptive to new truths,
And eager in the quest for knowledge—

For only thus shall they become lovers of and
seekers after truth.

Let this be our dream for our children:
That, day by day, they may find themselves, with
our help, more and more free

To make their own mistakes, and profit by them;
To discover their own values, and grow by them;
To reject our ways and adopt their own, and mature
by so doing—

For only thus shall they become better persons
than we have been.

Let this be our dream for our children:
That in their later years—and ours—
They may honor their fathers and mothers, and
other elders,
Not through some onerous sense of duty,

But with a sincere affection,
Born of the fact that no act of ours
Placed fetters on their truest freedom
Of mind and spirit and person.

Humbly, hopefully, devotedly,
We dream these dreams for our children;

And may ours be the sobering knowledge
That only through *our deeds*
Can all these dreams come true.

Amen

WILLIAM D. HAMMOND

*Frankly, though, there's no easy answer. Whatever
course you take—permissive or strict—it's a case of
damned if you do, damned if you don't. Dr. Howard
A. Lang, Professor of Education at New York Uni-
versity, sums up our frustration neatly: "Once we
blamed the devil, then the tonsils, then the I. Q., and
now the parents."*

Our own mothers warned us there'd be days like these. Remember how often your mother sighed, "Just wait until you have children of your own, then you'll understand!"? That was a prediction to cover every contingency. Yet though we laugh about it, suddenly there is much that we do understand. Now that we are mothers we are more and more aware of a kinship with the shadowy figures of the past, the long, long line of women who came before.

MARY LOVED LILACS

Mary loved lilacs in long-ago Virginia,
In Saint John's Parish on Mattaponi River;
Loved them for the fragrance of fog in their blos-
     soms—English fog.

Jemima and Joseph drove a Conestoga wagon
To frontier Kentucky. He took his ax and his
Bull-tongued plow, and she the walnut cradle
    And lilac roots.

Sarilda toiled the wilderness trail with her husband
To the muddy Missouri; planted a garden
Through ashes of council fires—lilacs, peonies,
    And damask roses.

Margaret followed Jim where the winds westward
    beckoned
Across the wild plains and the wolf-toothed Rockies;
Grubbed away sagebrush to stir in the red earth
    Seeds of home.

Mary, Jemima, Sarilda, and Margaret—
Deeply your roots bound America together.
Give me faith to plant, by the trial of strange to-
morrows,
My lilacs!

LULITA CRAWFORD PRITCHETT

*We are conscious of this new awareness in small
gestures of our own that we had not noticed before.*

WOMAN AT WINDOW

No volition sent her toward the window.
Indeed, she never knew
That she was standing there and staring.
Till something brought her to.

Then, with a pang, she suddenly remembered
How her mother used to be:
So often, hand to cheek, and staring, staring
At things *she* didn't see.

DOROTHY ALDIS

*This kinship with mothers who have gone before
may even result in a new reverence for family treasures we might have rejected haughtily had they been
offered early in our marriage.*

BEQUEST

"Dear Jane," the letter ran, "you'll find herein
The afghan willed to you, my next of kin:
Two yards of woven woes, a square for each,
For times when knitting helped things more than
    speech!
I drove the buggy up to town for yarn
When summer lightning struck and burned the
    barn;
And started knitting squares those nights I found
That Nate was squiring city girls around.
One whole row's the year when constant rain
Spoiled all our crops and flattened standing grain.
'Twas comforting to work that center square
The day a spavin lamed our sorrel mare;
And when our first-born, Andrew, ran away,
I knit together things I could not say.
The corner piece I finished up and tied
The night I sat alone when Nathan died.
It's something, though, I wanted you to keep:
My record of the times I did not weep.
You'll find it long on warmth, but short on looks!
With love, your Great-Aunt Temperance Esta-
    brooks."

DOROTHY H. HUGHES

*I never read about or see a coverlet of long ago but
I remember the patch work quilt, feather-stitched
with black yarn, that Aunt Gerty used to cover me
when I was sick and very, very small. And I never
recall the quilt without thinking of this poem:*

PATCHWORK

Life's moments might become a quilt at that,
If one would piece them, fitting as they will
While kettles boil, when neighbors sit and chat,
Or reading by the fire on evenings chill.

Oh, blessed simple things that make life sweet—
Those daisies growing golden in the sun,
A baby's gurgle, playing with his feet,
Or someone's eager step when day is done.

The flash of wings outside an open door,
Life's colored moments, prismlike they seem,
If one could piece them—comforts, laid in store
For bleaker days . . . to warm us while we dream!

EDNA JONES MARTIN

The sad fact is that life's moments are becoming more crowded day by day, with less and less time for dreaming. Especially if, by now, another child has come along. But in some ways it is easier with the second baby, isn't it? Now that we are old hands at this mother business, we can be calmer and more relaxed.

A young mother of four confessed: "When I had my first baby, I phoned the doctor every time he sneezed. My youngest swallowed a nickel the other day. I just looked at him and said: 'Young man, that money comes out of your allowance!' "

LAURA BERGQUIST

Reprinted from *Look* Magazine

Such a sense of humor can be the saving grace that sustains us through those days when one child plus one child seems to equal five. There's no denying it: more children equals more work. But surely it is as soul-satisfying work as any we will ever find— even when we are rewarded with moments of sentimental tenderness that backfire slightly.

HOW WE KEPT MOTHER'S DAY

One year our family decided to have a special celebration of Mother's Day, as a token of appreciation for all the sacrifices that Mother had made for us. After breakfast we had arranged, as a surprise, to hire a car and take her for a beautiful drive in the country. Mother was rarely able to have a treat like that, because she was busy in the house nearly all the time. But on the very morning of the day, we changed the plan a little, because it occurred to Father that it would be even better to take Mother fishing. As the car was hired and paid for, we might as well use it to drive up into the hills where the streams are. As Father said, if you just go driving you have a sense of aimlessness, but if you are going to fish there is a definite purpose that heightens the enjoyment.

So we all felt it would be nicer for Mother to have a definite purpose; and anyway, Father had just got a new rod the day before, which he said Mother could use if she wanted to; only Mother said she would much rather watch him fish than try to fish herself.

So we got her to make up a sandwich lunch in case we got hungry, though of course we were to come home again to a big festive dinner.

Well, when the car came to the door, it turned out that there wasn't as much room in it as we had supposed, because we hadn't reckoned on Father's fishing gear and the lunch, and it was plain that we couldn't all get in.

Father said not to mind him, that he could just as well stay home and put in the time working in the garden. He said that we were not to let the fact that he had not had a real holiday for three years stand in our way; he wanted us to go right ahead and not to mind him.

But of course we all felt that it would never do to let Father stay home, especially as we knew he would make trouble if he did. The two girls, Anna and Mary, would have stayed and gotten dinner, only it seemed such a pity to, on a lovely day like this, having their new hats. But they said that Mother had only to say the word and they'd gladly stay home and work. Will and I would have dropped out, but we wouldn't have been any use in getting the dinner.

So in the end it was decided that Mother would stay home and just have a lovely restful day around the house, and get the dinner. Also it turned out to be just a bit raw out-of-doors, and Father said he would never forgive himself if he dragged Mother round the country and let her take a severe cold. He said it was our duty to let Mother get all the rest and quiet she could, after all she had done for all of us, and that young people seldom realize how much quiet means to people who are getting old.

He could still stand the racket, but he was glad to shelter Mother from it.

Well, we had the loveliest day up among the hills, and Father caught such big specimens that he felt sure Mother couldn't have landed them anyway, if she had been fishing for them. Will and I fished too, and the two girls met some young men friends along the stream, and so we all had a splendid time.

We sat down to a roast turkey when we got back. Mother had to get up a good bit during the meal fetching things, but at the end Father said she simply mustn't do it, that he wanted her to spare herself, and he got up and fetched the walnuts from the sideboard himself.

The dinner was great fun, and when it was over all of us wanted to help clear the things up and wash the dishes, only Mother said that she would really much rather do it, and so we let her, because we wanted to humor her.

It was late when it was all over, and when we kissed Mother before going to bed, she said it had been the most wonderful day in her life, and I think there were tears in her eyes.

STEPHEN LEACOCK

Ah, the joys and rewards of motherhood!

Yet it's not just sentimentality to feel that all the tasks of rearing children and making a home can be transformed when viewed as labors of love. Take dishwashing for instance, the drudgery Mrs. Billy Graham most detests. She has tacked this poem above her kitchen sink:

KITCHEN PRAYER

Lord of all pots and pans, and things,
Since I've not time to be
A saint by doing lovely things
Or watching late with Thee,
Or dreaming in the dawn light,
Or storming heaven's gates,
Make me a saint by getting meals
And washing up the plates.

Warm all the kitchen with Thy love
And light it with Thy peace.
Forgive me all my worry,
And make my grumbling cease.
Thou who didst love to give men food,
In room or by the sea,
Accept this service that I do.
I do it unto Thee.

KLARA MUNKRES

Delightfully frank woman that she is, Mrs. Graham admits her problem isn't completely solved, but the therapy has helped. Perhaps a similar poem prominently displayed would soften the grind of . . . well, of mending, for one thing.

MENDED THINGS

Is it so strange that I love mended things:
A sock heel like a fine embroidered square,
A chair to which another era clings,

A plate so cherished that the utmost care
Was taken to preserve the fragments of it,
A little wagon nearly good as new
Again for owners who have grown to love it,
And always dolls with magic wrought by glue;
Old garden walls, and fences twice as stout
Now as the day the cattle wandered out,
And roads, and bridges, and each human tie
Of understanding, faith that seemed to shatter,
And love that longed to have another try?
Nothing is mended well that does not matter.

ELAINE V. EMANS

*That's all it takes, on many too-busy days, to bring
order out of chaos—just a word or two of inspiration.
Try these at the end of a weary hour:*

But they that wait upon the Lord shall renew
their strength; they shall mount up with wings as
eagles; they shall run and not be weary; they shall
walk and not faint.

ISAIAH 40:31

*Or as a last resort, if all else fails to ease the burden
of these often over-hectic days, we can try rolling up
our sleeves and wading right into the myriad tasks.
Of course it's work, being a homemaker, but who's
afraid of a little hard work?*

Manual labor to my father was not only good and decent for its own sake, but, as he was given to saying, it straightened out one's thoughts, a contention which I have since proved on many occasions. To scrub a floor has alleviated many a broken heart and to wash and iron one's clothes brought order and clarity to many a perplexed and anxious mind.

MARY ELLEN CHASE

And there is this redeeming feature in housework: you have so much to show for your effort when you're through!

HOME

What satisfaction warms my heart when all my
    house is clean!
That "there-it's-done-at-last-thank-heaven" feeling's
    what I mean.
How light, how free, how full of joy, how happy is
    the day!
There's every speck of dust swept up and smudges
    scrubbed away,
The furniture is polished to a soft, dark, perfect
    gleam;
The windows hold a sparkle and the curtains are a
    dream.
The corners shout: "Inspect us! We're the house-
    wife's little pride!"
The cupboards say: "We're spotless! Won't you
    have a look inside?"

81

No cobwebs, splatters, fingermarks, no footprints
    on the floor,
No grease, no grime—

Excuse me. There's a racket at the door. . . .
Boy in torn twill longies. Girl in red plaid skirt.
Man with pipe. Small brownish dog. *Family*. Dirt!

SHIRLEY SHAPIRO PUGH

But if more children mean more work, they mean
more fun, too, more laughter in the house, more joy.

THOUGH RAIN MAY FALL

The rain beats on my window sill,
It clatters in the street
But safe within my house I hear
The patter of young feet—
Of children running up the stair,
Of children running down,
Their spirits never dampened by
The storm that strikes the town.

Though lightning flashes, thunder roars
And branches lash about,
I listen for the sudden flash
Of laughter ringing out;
I listen for the thunder noise
Of children safe at play
With carefree voices shouting out
In their excited way.

What matter if the thunder rolls
And rain comes falling after

If I can keep within my house
The warm sun of their laughter.

HELEN HOWLAND PROMMEL

*But it's only in the morning that a mother can be so
philosophical! By afternoon of a rainy day your
thoughts are not so serene.*

DAY'S END

Our living room at evening takes on a mongrel air,
Without a sign of pedigree or mark of morning care.

Exactitude has perished beneath the evening feet
And disarray has entered with vigor from the street.

Its lampshades angle strangely; its curtains seem
    awry;
And yet it cocks a friendly ear and blinks a peaceful
    eye.

It wags indeed a livelier tail, the voice too big, per-
    haps.
Yet wholesomer, I will admit, than soft, anemic
    yaps.

Papa and paper fill one chair, daughter and dolls,
    the floor.
Son and sounds are going the rounds, which Mama
    must ignore.

And cozily at bedtime, unmindful of its flaws,
It slumbers as it pleases with litter round its paws.

ISABELLE BRYANS LONGFELLOW

But no rainy day lasts forever (it just seems that way). Tomorrow, with luck, the sun will shine and your noisy darlings can be shooed out into the garden.

QUITE CONTRARY

I have a garden that isn't a garden.
It's just where the children have somewhere to play.
There are curious scratches and bare, earthy patches
The pup likes to dig in and hide bones away.

I have a garden that isn't a garden.
The phlox and the hollyhock grow, to be sure,
In weedy profusion in spite of confusion;
But only the sturdiest plants can endure.

I have a garden; it isn't a garden
That Flower Show people would ever pick out,
For I have a theory, disorder is cheery,
And like to see growing things running about.

SARA KING CARLETON

I can't think of any philosophy more conducive to serenity than the theory that "disorder is cheery." And surely, if we hope to take motherhood in our stride, we might just as well become resigned to seeing growing things (especially children) running about.

THE DEFINITION OF A MOTHER

Do you know that Webster defines a mother as "a female parent"? This is the understatement of all time, and I'd like to tell Mr. Webster why his description should be revised.

A mother is a walking encyclopedia who is expected to know Stan Musial's batting average, how to tie a half hitch, and where somebody left last Sunday's comics. She must answer unhesitatingly such questions as where the sun goes at night, how jet propulsion works, what the principal exports of Thailand are, and where baby kittens come from.

A mother is a master mechanic who can get a trouser leg out of a bicycle chain, and can fix anything with cellophane tape and a hairpin. She is a plumber who knows that the water won't run out of the bathtub because the tissue-paper sails have come off the children's boats and are clogging the drain. She is an electrician who can make the electric train back up without blowing a fuse.

On days when a lemonade stand appears on the front lawn, a mother is the supply sergeant who never runs out of lemons. She has an endless supply of sharpened pencils and bandages on hand, and a drawer full of presents for the birthday parties her children have been invited to but have forgotten to tell her about.

A mother is a practical nurse who knows how to make a splint for a bird's broken wing. She must also be able to remove splinters and loose teeth painlessly, stop an earache in the middle of the night, and cure a case of measles before the fourth-grade picnic.

A mother is a detective who finds the missing

mate to every sock. When her scissors and flashlight disappear, she can recover them long before the culprits plead guilty.

A mother is an untiring seamstress who sews on Scout badges, designs tricky patches for jeans, replaces lost buttons, and lets down and takes up dozens of hems. She must also be able to make such a beautiful halo and pair of wings that the school-play audience will never notice that the angel's two front teeth are missing.

She must be an industrial designer who can decorate a tricycle that will win a prize in the Fourth of July parade.

She is a mathematician who doubles and triples recipes in a split second when her daughter asks the whole neighborhood to lunch. Her bookkeeping must be accurate enough to keep track of overdrawn allowances, Christmas-fund borrowings and hours owed for dishwashing assignments.

She must be a psychologist who knows why the baby won't eat his spinach, that the boy who hates girls is going to ask one to go square dancing Friday night, and that the proudly displayed drawing of a scribbled blot with legs happens to be a cow.

A mother is a diplomat who convinces her skeptical child that *Snow White* will be much more entrancing than *The Devil Men from Mars*. She must be a mind reader who knows how many friends her youngest has invited to his birthday party, and whether her eldest is going to want to use the car a week from Wednesday.

She must be an athlete—old enough to remember how to do the Charleston, but not too old to play hide-and-seek.

86

She is a sage who is wise enough to know when her son has reached the age at which he would rather die than be kissed in public, and when her daughter's best friend has won the admiration of the only boy in the world. Yet she is also an innocent who never ceases to wonder at the miracle of life when the first crocus peeks through the snow and the first blue egg appears in a robin's nest.

A mother is a lady in waiting who is never too busy to help look for a lost ball, too tired to read another story aloud, or too squeamish to bait a hook with a wriggling worm.

A mother is an heiress! Although she may not feel wealthy when she is trying to stretch the family budget to include braces on teeth and dancing lessons, she is rich in rewards. She is rich in the pride that engulfs her when her teen-ager offers to mow the neighbors' lawn while they are away on vacation, or her Little Leaguer insists on pitching with a sprained finger rather than let his teammates down. She is rich in investments: As she watches her small daughter tenderly tucking her doll into bed, she hopes her child will grow up to know the happiness of being a mother.

It is then that she knows, Mr. Webster, that a mother deserves the longest definition in the world!

LOUISE SHATTUCK

And there are respites from the din. Every mother has her favorite time of the day, the time when all the labor seems worthwhile.

87

EVENING NEWS FLASH

Snap shut the dial. Evening floods the room
Suddenly with the small, familiar noise
Of clattering pots, a slammed screen door, the zoom
Of roller skates, bearing the neighbors' boys
In wild, swift cavalcade, intent to meet
Homecoming steps along the quiet street.

Listen: the outraged air forgets the news.
A lawn mower's drone, a mother's supper call,
The simple sound effects all suburbs use
Drift on the evening breeze. And that is all—
That strange, sweet sound of living, free of fear,
Making a music God leans down to hear.

BROOKE BYRNE

Such peaceful interludes make hectic days worthwhile. But the evil of all this work lies, not in the effort itself, but in the possibility that it may warp our sense of values, make us too busy for the things that matter most.

LOST OCTOBER

There never comes a day like this, all gold
And shining like a bubble in the sun,
But I recall the afternoon I told
You I'd no time for play: work must be done!
Work must be done, and there the gold day wasted,
And there the mellowness of earth and sky
And leaf and air went hour by hour untasted
For scruples sown too well in such as I!

And there October's brightness faded, turning
Her dear enchantment into dull November,
And setting in my brain one question burning:
Now what can I, now what can I remember
Of work I bent above that day until
It was too late to climb the golden hill?

ELAINE V. EMANS

*We might be wise to tack these lines above the
kitchen stove some bright spring morning:*

REBELLION

What is there to be hurrying for?
　　Why should I scurry and worry?
The fluff of blankets will make the floor
　　In a hundred years as furry,

In a hundred years the stars and moons
　　Will turn in their ancient courses,
And there'll be tarnish on silver spoons
　　And moths'll still marshal forces.

In a hundred years the sun will shine
　　And bumblebees will bumble,
And the wind will plunge in the hillside pine
　　And weeds will be gay and humble.

But I won't be here! Let blankets shed
　　Their fuzz all over the place,
Under the bureau, under the bed—
　　I'll run myself a race:

I'll go with today across the grass
   And up the hill and over
And lift my heart where high winds pass
   And lie in the buds of clover.

In a hundred years the sun will burn
   And I shall be asleep,
But I shall have felt the great earth turn
   And have today to keep.

FRANCES FROST

*I can't recall who wrote it, but how true this old
rhyme still is:*

Tomorrow some will never see;
Yesterday no more will be;
All we're sure of is today—
Why, then, throw the chance away?

THE DAY WE FLEW THE KITES

"String!" shouted Brother, bursting into the kitchen.
"We need lots more string."

It was Saturday. As always, it was a busy one, for
"Six days shalt thou labor and do all thy work" was
taken seriously then. Outside, Father and Mr. Patrick next door were doing chores.

Inside the two houses, Mother and Mrs. Patrick
were engaged in spring cleaning. Such a windy
March day was ideal for "turning out" clothes
closets. Already woolens flapped on back-yard
clotheslines.

Somehow the boys had slipped away to the back lot with their kites. Now, even at the risk of having Brother impounded to beat carpets, they had sent him for more string. Apparently there was no limit to the heights to which kites would soar today.

My mother looked out the window. The sky was piercingly blue; the breeze fresh and exciting. Up in all that blueness sailed puffy billows of clouds. It had been a long, hard winter, but today was Spring.

Mother looked at the sitting room, its furniture disordered for a Spartan sweeping. Again her eyes wavered toward the window. "Come on, girls! Let's take string to the boys and watch them fly the kites a minute." On the way we met Mrs. Patrick, laughing guiltily, escorted by her girls.

There never was such a day for flying kites! God doesn't make two such days in a century. We played all our fresh twine into the boys' kites and still they soared. We could hardly distinguish the tiny, orange-colored specks. Now and then we slowly reeled one in, finally bringing it dipping and tugging to earth, for the sheer joy of sending it up again. What a thrill to run with them, to the right, to the left, and see our poor, earth-bound movements reflected minutes later in the majestic sky-dance of the kites! We wrote wishes on slips of paper and slipped them over the string. Slowly, irresistibly, they climbed up until they reached the kites. Surely all such wishes would be granted!

Even our fathers dropped hoe and hammer and joined us. Our mothers took their turn, laughing like schoolgirls. Their hair blew out of their pompadours and curled loose about their cheeks; their gingham aprons whipped about their legs. Mingled with our fun was something akin to awe. The grown-ups were really playing with us! Once I looked at Mother and thought she looked actually pretty. And her over forty!

We never knew where the hours went on that hilltop day. There were no hours, just a golden, breezy Now. I think we were all a little beyond ourselves. Parents forgot their duty and their dignity; children forgot their combativeness and small spites. "Perhaps it's like this in the Kingdom of Heaven," I thought confusedly.

It was growing dark before, drunk with sun and air, we all stumbled sleepily back to the houses. I suppose we had some sort of supper. I suppose there must have been a surface tidying-up, for the house on Sunday looked decorous enough.

The strange thing was, we didn't mention that day afterward. I felt a little embarrassed. Surely none of the others had thrilled to it as deeply as I. I locked the memory up in that deepest part of me where we keep "the things that cannot be and yet are."

The years went on, then one day I was scurrying about my own kitchen in a city apartment, trying to get some work out of the way while my three-year-old insistently cried her desire to "go park and see ducks."

"I *can't* go!" I said. "I have this and this to do, and when I'm through I'll be too tired to walk that far."

My mother, who was visiting us, looked up from the peas she was shelling. "It's a wonderful day," she offered; "really warm, yet there's a fine, fresh breeze. It reminds me of that day we flew the kites."

I stopped in my dash between stove and sink. The locked door flew open, and with it a gush of memories. I pulled off my apron. "Come on," I told my little girl. "You're right, it's too good a day to miss."

Another decade passed. We were in the aftermath of a great war. All evening we had been asking our returned soldier, the youngest Patrick boy, about his experiences as a prisoner of war. He had talked freely, but now for a long time he had been silent. What was he thinking of—what dark and dreadful things?

"Say!" A smile twitched his lips. "Do you remember . . . no, of course you wouldn't. It probably didn't make the impression on you it did on me."

I hardly dared speak. "Remember what?"

"I used to think of that day a lot in PW camp, when things weren't too good. Do you remember the day we flew the kites?"

Winter came, and the sad duty of a call of condolence on Mrs. Patrick, recently widowed. I dreaded the call. I couldn't imagine how Mrs. Patrick would face life alone.

We talked a little of my family and her grandchildren and the changes in the town. Then she was silent, looking down at her lap. I cleared my throat. Now I must say something about her loss, and she would begin to cry.

When she looked up, Mrs. Patrick was smiling, "I was just sitting here thinking," she said. "Henry had such fun that day. Frances, do you remember the day we flew the kites?"

FRANCES FOWLER

Haven't you often observed that by some obscure law of arithmetic—or of human nature—the larger the family, the larger the store of such warm, wonderful memories? Yet a large family presents problems that the mother of an only child need never face. The fear of showing favoritism, for example, is ever present.

A New York social worker asked a client, who was raising a healthy, wholesome family of ten in the East Side slums, "But isn't there one you really love the best?" And the mother answered, "Yes. The one who is sick until he gets well; the one who's away, until he gets home."

From the children's standpoint, there are wondrous advantages in having a sister or a brother.

DOUBLE BOY

Snow was heavy on the world,
   Pines bowed under white,
Children were wading home from school
   Along the wall of night.

A man trudged up a breakneck hill
   And overtook a queer
Double creature, that turned out
   Two boys as he came near.

One boy staggered, legs apart,
   One rode with knees still wider,

The walker did not look a year
    Wider than the rider.

As far's the man could see, the legs
    Were hardly half-past eight,
The upper half was a butterball
    Of live and curving weight.

Their only double parts, their seats,
    Were twins for cloth and size.
The upper boy was head and back,
    The lower boy just thighs.

The man sang out to him: "It's good
    For boys to help each other.
But isn't that an awful load?"
    "No, sir. It's my brother!"

                ROBERT P. TRISTRAM COFFIN

*The child who has a brother or sister is never again
wholly alone. Together they are allies against the
alien adult world that would dominate them.*

FRIENDSHIP

OH, THE COMFORT—the inexpressible comfort of feel-
    ing safe with a person,
Having neither to weigh thoughts,
Nor measure words—but pouring them
All right out—just as they are—
Chaff and grain together—
Certain that a faithful hand will
Take and sift them—
Keep what is worth keeping—

95

And with the breath of kindness
Blow the rest away.

DINAH MARIA MULOCK CRAIK

Now and again, we could do with a little of such comfort and understanding, couldn't we?

OCCUPATION: HOUSEWIFE

After planning, marketing, cooking, after
Scouring the house from cellar to rafter,

After the dinner dishes are done
And the children disposed of, one by one,

After a day as domestic pearls,
We're supposed to turn into glamour girls,

Lovely and well worth a husband's wooing.
And it can't be done—and that's what we're doing!

MAY RICHSTONE

But if you are inclined to moan that our fast-paced modern life is the villain, that grandma had it easier, just consider these specifications for a model wife in Biblical times.

A woman of valour who can find?
For her price is far above rubies.
The heart of her husband doth safely trust in her,

96

And he hath no lack of gain.
She doeth him good and not evil
All the days of her life.
She seeketh wool and flax,
And worketh willingly with her hands.
She is like the merchant-ships;
She bringeth her food from afar.
She riseth also while it is yet night,
And giveth food to her household,
And a portion to her maidens.
She considereth a field, and buyeth it;
With the fruit of her hands she planteth a vineyard.
She girdeth her loins with strength,
And maketh strong her arms.
She perceiveth that her merchandise is good;
Her lamp goeth not out by night.
She layeth her hands to the distaff,
And her hands hold the spindle.
She stretcheth out her hand to the poor;
Yea, she reacheth forth her hands to the needy.
She is not afraid of the snow for her household;
For all her household are clothed with scarlet.
She maketh for herself coverlets;
Her clothing is fine linen and purple.
Her husband is known in the gates,
When he sitteth among the elders of the land.
She maketh linen garments and selleth them;
And delivereth girdles unto the merchant.
Strength and dignity are her clothing;
And she laugheth at the time to come.
She openeth her mouth with wisdom;
And the law of kindness is on her tongue.
She looketh well to the ways of her household,
And eateth not the bread of idleness.
Her children rise up, and call her blessed;

Her husband also, and he praiseth her:
"Many daughters have done valiantly,
But thou excellest them all."
Grace is deceitful, and beauty is vain;
But a woman that feareth the LORD, she shall be
    praised.
Give her of the fruit of her hands;
And let her works praise her in the gates.

PROVERBS 31:10–31

*If that excerpt from the Holy Scriptures has embued
you with a striving toward perfection, surely you
could aim for no higher goal than this:*

Lord, make me an instrument of Thy peace; where
there is hatred, let me sow love; where there is
doubt, faith; where there is despair, hope; where
there is darkness, light; and where there is sadness,
joy.

O Divine Master, grant that I may not so much
seek to be consoled as to console; to be understood,
as to understand; to be loved, as to love; for it is in
giving that we receive, it is in pardoning that we are
pardoned, and it is in dying that we are born to
eternal life.

ST. FRANCIS OF ASSISI

*But if, in these hectic, crowded days when the chil-
dren are small and demanding, if in these hectic days
we often fall short of perfection, surely we can take*

98

comfort in the instinctive knowledge that He is
generous in His judgments.

GOD TO A MOTHER

Do not fear
To nod your head a bit.
Lean back and sit
Comfortably, here against the pew.
You had so many things to do
About the house
Before you came:
There was the baby's bath,
There was the game
Of dominoes you straightened out
For Dick and Bill.
Your hands are still
Trembling from rushing so
Before the time for you to go.
Relax and rest a bit
Now, as you sit
Before my sanctuary.
You are so very tired.
What if you miss a word or two?
It is no sin. Oh, have no fear!
It is enough that you are here.

MYRTLE VORST SHEPPARD

Dark Days

For even the most dedicated mothers there come days that go far beyond the merely hectic. Days when we honestly don't see how we can keep going any longer. Often the trouble is just plain fatigue. On such a day, bone-tired and limp with weariness, I found this poem. It helped me through that day and many a dark day since.

FOUR O'CLOCK

There is a time for coffee and for wine,
But tea is more than these: A cup of tea
Is not so much a drink as it's a mood—
Tea is for comfort. Tired of motion, speech,
And too much living, needing a retreat,
One seeks a corner out of the world's reach;
Then is the time to brew a cup of tea.

Tea is a kind hand upon the head,
A voice that says, "There, there,"
The necessary step between despair
And what's to be done next.
Tea is philosophy.

PAULA COFFEY GILBERT

That philosophy can unlock a secret source of strength; a quiet pause in a day so busy that any rest seems sinful. Perhaps we can pass the secret of that wonderful restorer along to our own children, to brighten the dark days their futures may hold.

A LITTLE PIECE OF LIGHT

When I was of bicycle age I knew a woman who had more troubles than anyone else in town. Her children were a laboratory for accident and disease; her own health teetered continuously on the edge; her husband was an inept man who could stumble over his own feet and believe he had been tripped. Yet none of this misery seemed to afflict her disposition. Her hair turned white and her face became thin, but her eyes stayed bright and when she smiled the air around her filled with something that felt like a warm sweater on a cold day.

I often carried medicines to her from the drugstore. One day after I had expressed sympathy for her latest misfortune, I said, before I could stop myself, "Gosh, ma'am, how do you stand it?"

She turned her smile on me. "I have a secret helper," she said. "I was raised on a farm, with three younger brothers. My mother had the care of all of us, and lots of farm work besides. When I was seven, on a freezing winter afternoon things got worse than ever. A cow was ailing, the water pump froze, and two of my brothers were sick. I was frantic with worry for my mother, and determined to help her. I came into the kitchen carrying a pail which I had filled with snow to melt for water to wash the dishes.

"My mother looked at the pail of snow and began to laugh. Then she cried a little. Then she kissed me, took me by the hand and said, 'You and I are going to sit down and have a cup of tea together.'

"She made tea from the snow water, and we sat at the kitchen table and drank it. It was my first cup of tea.

"That is my secret helper—that scene in the kitchen. Whenever I feel discouraged or very tired, I think of it, and I begin to laugh, and then to cry a little—it's good to cry now and then—and I sit down and make myself a cup of tea. When it's finished I'm ready to pull my apron tight and get on with what needs to be done."

She turned from the door. "Come in. We'll have a cup together right now." When I left she pushed her fingers through my hair and said, "A happy memory is the most valuable thing in the world."

THOMAS SUGRUE

When it is more than weariness that is depressing us, perhaps it's cabin fever, a disease to which we mothers are particularly susceptible in the early

years—four walls closing it, never anyone older than
four to talk with. There are days when we ask, is it
worth it? but of course we know it is. Anne Camp-
bell, in one of the loveliest little verses ever written
for a daughter, has said . . .

You are the trip I did not take.
You are the pearls I cannot buy.
You are my blue Italian lake.
You are my piece of foreign sky.

There never was a mother yet who raised her young-
sters without tears. Either you've learned that by
now or you will, someday!

AN ANCIENT GESTURE

I thought, as I wiped my eyes on the corner of my
    apron:
Penelope did this too
And more than once. You can't keep weaving all
    day
And undoing it all through the night;
Your arms get tired, and the back of your neck gets
    tight;
And along towards morning, when you think it will
    never be light,
And your husband has been gone, and you don't
    know where, for years,
Suddenly you burst into tears;
    There is simply nothing else to do.

And I thought, as I wiped my eyes on the corner of
    my apron:
This is an ancient gesture, authentic, antique,
In the very best tradition, classic, Greek;
Ulysses did this too.
But only as a gesture, a gesture which implied
To the assembled throng that he was much too
    moved to speak.
He learned it from Penelope . . .
    Penelope, who really cried.

                    EDNA ST. VINCENT MILLAY

*But a mother cannot always afford the luxury of
tears. Sometimes she must find the strength to stand
dry-eyed against her grief. Someone in every family
must face the really dark days with head high and
voice steady. Mothers seem supremely fitted for the
task.*

MAMA AND HER BANK ACCOUNT

For as long as I could remember, the small cottage
on Castro Street had been home. The familiar background was there; Mama, Papa, my only brother,
Nels. There was my sister Christine, closest to me
in age, yet ever secret and withdrawn—and the littlest sister, Dagmar.

There, too, came the Aunts, Mama's four sisters.
Aunt Jenny, who was the oldest and the bossiest;
Aunt Sigrid; Aunt Marta; and our maiden Aunt,
Trina.

The Aunts' old bachelor uncle, my Great-Uncle Chris—the "black Norwegian"—came with his great impatience, his shouting and stamping. And brought mystery and excitement to our humdrum days.

But the first awareness was of Mama.

I remember that every Saturday night Mama would sit down by the scrubbed kitchen table and with much wrinkling of usually placid brows count out the money Papa had brought home in the little envelope.

There would be various stacks.

"For the landlord," Mama would say, piling up the big silver pieces.

"For the grocer." Another group of coins.

"For Katrin's shoes to be half-soled." And Mama would count out the little silver.

"Teacher says this week I'll need a notebook." That would be Christine or Nels or I.

Mama would solemnly detach a nickel or a dime and set it aside.

We would watch the diminishing pile with breathless interest.

At last, Papa would ask, "Is all?"

And when Mama nodded, we could relax a little and reach for schoolbooks and homework. For Mama would look up then and smile. "Is good," she'd murmur. "We do not have to go to the Bank."

It was a wonderful thing, that Bank Account of Mama's. We were all so proud of it. It gave us such a warm, secure feeling. No one else we knew had money in a big bank downtown.

I remember when the Jensens down the street were put out because they couldn't pay their rent. We children watched the big strange men carry out the furniture, took furtive notice of poor Mrs. Jensen's shamed tears, and I was choked with sudden fear. This, then, happened to people who did not have the stack of coins marked "Landlord." Might this, could this, violence happen to us?

I clutched Christine's hands. "*We* have a Bank Account," she reassured me calmly, and suddenly I could breathe again.

When Nels graduated from grammar school he wanted to go on to High. "Is good," Mama said, and Papa nodded approvingly.

"It will cost a little money," Nels said.

Eagerly we brought up chairs and gathered around the table. I took down the gaily painted box that Aunt Sigrid had sent us from Norway one Christmas and laid it carefully in front of Mama.

This was the "Little Bank." Not to be confused, you understand, with the big Bank downtown. The "Little Bank" was used for sudden emergencies, such as the time Christine broke her arm and had to be taken to a doctor, or when Dagmar got croup and Papa had to go to the drugstore for medicine to put into the steam kettle.

Nels had it all written out neatly. So much for carfare, for clothes, for notebooks and supplies. Mama looked at the figures for a long time. Then she counted out the money in the Little Bank. There was not enough.

She pursed her lips. "We do not," she reminded us gently, "want to have to go to the Bank."

We all shook our heads.

"I will work in Dillon's grocery after school," Nels volunteered.

Mama gave him a bright smile and laboriously wrote down a sum and added and subtracted. Papa did it in his head. He was very quick on arithmetic. "Is not enough," he said. Then he took his pipe out of his mouth and looked at it for a long time. "I give up tobacco," he said suddenly.

Mama reached across the table and touched Papa's sleeve, but she didn't say anything. Just wrote down another figure.

"I will mind the Elvington children every Friday night," I said. "Christine can help me."

We all felt very good. We had passed another milestone without having to go downtown and draw money out of Mama's Bank Account. The Little Bank was sufficient for the present.

So many things, I remember, came out of the Little Bank that year. Christine's costume for the school play, Dagmar's tonsil operation, my Girl Scout uniform. And always, in the background, was the comforting knowledge that should our efforts fail, we still had the Bank to depend upon.

Even when the Strike came, Mama would not let us worry unduly. We all worked together so that the momentous trip downtown could be postponed. It was almost like a game.

During that time Mama "helped out" at Kruper's bakery for a big sack of only slightly stale bread and coffeecake. And as Mama said, fresh bread was not too good for a person and if you put the coffeecake into the hot oven it was nearly as nice as when first baked.

Papa washed bottles at the Castro Creamery every night and they gave him three quarts of fresh milk and all the sour milk he could carry away. Mama made fine cheese.

The day the Strike was over and Papa went back

to work, I saw Mama stand a little straighter, as if to get a kink out of her back.

She looked around at us proudly. "Is *good*," she smiled. "See? We did not have to go down to the Bank."

That was twenty years ago.

Last year I sold my first story. When the check came I hurried over to Mama's and put the long green slip of paper in her lap. "For you," I said, "to put in your Bank Account."

And I noticed for the first time how old Mama and Papa looked. Papa seemed shorter, now, and Mama's wheaten braids were sheened with silver.

Mama fingered the check and looked at Papa.

"Is good," she said, and her eyes were proud.

"Tomorrow," I told her, "you must take it down to the Bank."

"You will go with me, Katrin?"

"That won't be necessary, Mama. See? I've endorsed the check to you. Just hand it to the teller, he'll deposit it to your account."

Mama looked at me. "Is no account," she said. "In all my life, I never been inside a Bank."

And when I didn't—couldn't—answer, Mama said earnestly: "Is not *good* for little ones to be afraid—to not feel secure."

KATHRYN FORBES

Mothers—not just Mama, but all mothers—are realists. The art of compromise, of half-a-loaf, is one at which we soon become adept.

THESE THINGS

Always a mountain that you cannot climb;
Always a rushing stream too wide to ford;
Always a losing battle against time;
Always a goal that you keep pushing toward;
Always a gamble that you dare not take;
Always a door that's fastened with a bar;
Always a love for which your heart must break—
These are the things that make you what you are.
These things (and not the treasures, easy-come, that fall
Into your hands) will make you great of soul—or small.

BEULAH FRANCES HOLLAND

With this philosophical attitude we dull the edge of our own disappointments, but it's another story when our children are hurt; then we operate on instinct, the tiger-protecting-her-cubs instinct.

It is not easy to be philosophical about our children's inevitable sorrows, but try we must:

Have you learned lessons only of those who admired you, and were tender with you, and stood aside for you? Have you not learned great lessons from those who braced themselves against you, and disputed the passage with you?

WALT WHITMAN

But what of the other blows Life deals them? What
of the pain that has no healing, the grief that teaches
no lesson except forbearance?

PROPOSED PACT

Last night, dear Lord, he dreamed that he was tall,
And oh, dear Lord, you should have seen his face
When telling me; you wouldn't guess at all
That he had shriveled legs or wore a brace,
For he sat up so straight, dear Lord, his eyes
Were like blue crystals in a velvet mask,
As he told how he stretched his legs to rise
To his new height; and so, dear Lord, I ask
A favor; You may smile at my request,
I've thought the whole thing through; can You ar-
    range
With him who deals out dreams at Your behest—
For my lad's broken dreams this fair exchange:
Let dark dreams fall to me, I'll take them all,
But give him back the dream that he was tall!

                          JESSIE FARNHAM

That is the ultimate tragedy compounded—hurt to
our children when we are powerless to help. When
things are really bad it's the nights that are the worst.
After all the alcohol sponge baths, after the last sip
of ice water from the angled glass straw, after the
fresh cool pillowcase, there is nothing left to do ex-
cept wait. Never are we so utterly alone as when we
watch by the bedside of a suffering child, listening
to his heavy breathing and to the faint night-sounds

*of the sleeping house. In the shadow of helplessness
and aloneness, panic swamps us, sweeps us almost to
the breaking point, unless we can seize in time upon
the nearness of God.*

> I falter where I firmly trod,
>   And falling with my weight of cares
>   Upon the great world's altar-stairs
> That slope thro' darkness up to God,
> I stretch lame hands of faith, and grope . . .

Eternal God, who hast been the hope and joy of
many generations, and who in all ages hast given
men the power to seek Thee and in seeking to find
Thee, grant me, I pray Thee, a clearer vision of Thy
truth, a greater faith in Thy power, and a more
confident assurance of Thy love.

When the way seems dark before me, give me grace
    to walk trustingly:
When much is obscure to me, let me be all the
    more faithful to the little that I can clearly see:
When the distant scene is clouded, let me rejoice
    that at least the next step is plain:
When what Thou art is most hidden from my eyes,
    let me still hold fast to what Thou dost com-
    mand:
When insight falters, let obedience stand firm:
What I lack in faith let me repay in love.

JOHN BAILLIE

*In the final analysis those are the only answers to the
dark days: faith and love. Faith can be our own*

shield; love is the shield we forge for our child. When love cannot shield, it can become a sword, a weapon to buttress a child's own courage.

She poured herself a sputtering-hot cup of black coffee and reflected about children. One would think the world might be ashamed to name such a day for one of them and then go on the same old way: children running the lanes, lost sheep crying in the wind. Lord save little children! Because with every child ever born of woman there is a time of running through a shadowed place, an alley with no doors, and a hunter whose footsteps ring brightly along the bricks behind him. With every child— rich or poor—there is this time of echoing and vast aloneness, when there is no one to come nor to hear, and dry leaves scurrying past along a street become the rustle of Dread and the ticking of the old house is the cocking of the hunter's gun. To Rachel the most moving thing of all had been her lifelong witnessing of the humbling grace with which these small ones accept their lot. Lord save little children! They would weep at a broken toy but stand with the courage of a burning saint before the murder of a mother. The death of a kitten would send them screaming to the handiest female lap and yet when the time came that they were no longer welcome in a house, they would gather their things together in old paper cartons tied with lengths of clothesline and wander forth to seek another street, another door. Lord save little children! For each of them has his Preacher to hound him down the dark river of fear and no ear to heed it if there were a word

and no one to understand it if it were heard. Lord
save little children! They abide and they endure.

DAVIS GRUBB

*Though we try to spare them the blackest of the dark
days, every mother knows she cannot smooth her
youngster's path forever. The wise mother wouldn't,
even if she could.*

I asked God for strength, that I might achieve—
   I was made weak, that I might learn humbly to
     obey.
I asked for help that I might do greater things—
   I was given infirmity, that I might do better
     things.
I asked for riches, that I might be happy—
   I was given poverty, that I might be wise.
I asked for all things, that I might enjoy life—
   I was given life, that I might enjoy all things.
I got nothing that I asked for—but everything I had
    hoped for.
Despite myself, my prayers were answered. I am,
    among all men, most richly blessed.

AN ANONYMOUS SOLDIER OF THE CONFEDERACY

*After just a little living in this world we see that what
seem to be obstacles—even tragedies—may open the
door to a richer and more meaningful life.*

Waiting for the pediatrician to give my husky three
their tetanus shots, I was attracted by the shy smile
of a tiny girl with a crutch beside her chair. "I'm

116

going to walk pretty soon," she confided. "The doctor just promised me!"

The door of the inner office opened and her mother came out leading a little boy whose arm was shriveled.

I was shocked. "The mother of those two has a really hard row to hoe," I said to the doctor when they had gone.

"She's one of the happiest people I know," he replied. "Interesting thing. She had a sorry childhood —her father in a mental hospital, her mother obsessed by the fear that his illness would be transmitted to the daughter. She met her husband on a train as she was going to visit her dad. His mother was a patient there, too. Later, when they wanted to be married, they came to me. I told them what I knew—darned little—and they decided to go ahead but never to have children. However, they asked me to help them adopt a baby—'Not a picture-book one, guaranteed perfect, but one with the cards stacked against it.'

"So I found Pete for them. A fine lad. When he was four, they found Meg. And they're going to have another child soon."

I stared at him. "You mean—?"

"As soon as Meg is walking, a kid who's been battling rheumatic fever all his life is joining them. They're raising the finest family in my whole practice."

MRS. WILLIAM WALLACE

But sorrow is not always imposed on a family from without. Some of our most poignant heartaches are those we create ourselves.

FATHER FORGETS—

Listen, son: I am saying this as you lie asleep, one little paw crumpled under your cheek and the blond curls stickily wet on your damp forehead. I have stolen into your room alone. Just a few minutes ago, as I sat reading my paper in the library, a stifling wave of remorse swept over me. Guiltily I came to your bedside.

These are the things I was thinking, son: I had been cross to you. I scolded you as you were dressing for school because you gave your face merely a dab with a towel. I took you to task for not cleaning your shoes. I called out angrily when you threw some of your things on the floor.

At breakfast I found fault, too. You spilled things. You gulped down your food. You put your elbows on the table. You spread butter too thick on your bread. And as you started off to play and I made for my train, you turned and waved a hand and called, "Good-by, Daddy!" and I frowned, and said in reply, "Hold your shoulders back!"

Then it began all over again in the late afternoon. As I came up the road I spied you, down on your knees, playing marbles. There were holes in your stockings. I humiliated you before your boy friends by marching you ahead of me to the house. Stockings were expensive—and if you had to buy them you would be more careful! Imagine that, son, from a father!

Do you remember, later, when I was reading in the library, how you came in, timidly, with a sort of hurt look in your eyes? When I glanced up over my paper, impatient at the interruption, you hesitated at the door. "What is it you want?" I snapped.

You said nothing, but ran across in one tempestuous plunge, and threw your arms around my neck and kissed me, and your small arms tightened with an affection that God had set blooming in your heart and which even neglect could not wither. And then you were gone, pattering up the stairs.

Well, son, it was shortly afterwards that my paper slipped from my hands and a terrible sickening fear came over me. What has habit been doing to me? The habit of finding fault, of reprimanding—this was my reward to you for being a boy. It was not that I did not love you; it was that I expected too much of youth. It was measuring you by the yardstick of my own years.

And there was so much that was good and fine and true in your character. The little heart of you was as big as the dawn itself over the wide hills. This was shown by your spontaneous impulse to rush in and kiss me good-night. Nothing else matters tonight, son. I have come to your bedside in the darkness, and I have knelt there, ashamed!

It is a feeble atonement; I know you would not understand these things if I told them to you during your waking hours. But tomorrow I will be a real daddy! I will chum you, and suffer when you suffer, and laugh when you laugh. I will bite my tongue when impatient words come. I will keep saying as if it were a ritual: "He is nothing but a boy—a little boy!"

I am afraid I have visualized you as a man. Yet as I see you now, son, crumpled and weary in your cot, I see that you are still a baby. Yesterday you were in your mother's arms, your head on her shoulder. I have asked too much, too much.

W. LIVINGSTON LARNED

But parents have no monopoly on misunderstanding! Any mother of more than one child soon learns that her offspring can dredge up enough recriminations, taunts, accusations, and slurs to manufacture their own dark days.

HOW TO ENJOY A FAMILY QUARREL

There are grounds for deep suspicion, I think, in the idea of a family group which does not occasionally dissolve itself into a mass of screaming squabblers. I know of families where no word of dissent is ever permitted before—or from—the children, and these tend to be families where no word of tenderness either is ever permitted before—or from—the children. Not to put too fine a point on it, if two or three or four or five or six people live together in one house, sooner or later something is going to come up about which they do not see eye to eye and are prepared to say so. The children are displeased with their parents, perhaps, or displeased with each other or some outside element; it is even possible that the parents are displeased with their children. It would surely be unsafe to imagine that the average family could keep these emotions safely unspoken without some damage to the psyche, particularly the parents'.

In our family we are six—two parents and four children—and we are given to what I might call unceasing differences of opinion, more or less violent. Almost any subject, from politics to small variations in daily dress, can find us lined up in formation on two bitterly opposed sides. Such a subject as "*Resolved*, That all allowances be trebled because of general charm and amiability" can keep us going for quite a while. This one is still current, my husband and I taking the negative.

We learned very early that it was safest to hold a united front on all major issues in front of the children. Since four of the members of our family are children, we also have learned never, never, *never* to put *anything* to a democratic vote. Time after time we found ourselves out-voted four to two and involved in things like going on a picnic tomorrow no matter whether it rains or not, and inviting those nice people with all the children to come for a weekend. Also we found out very early—when our older son was about six weeks old, in fact—that no parents ever got anywhere by calling in outsiders, particularly grandparents, for an impartial judgment.

Family arguments tend to be of two sorts, although one is not necessarily more peaceful than the other: the personal, or no-discussion-before-company type; and what for want of a better word might be called the impersonal—philosophical, political or moral questions from the world at large. (The situation in the Middle East, for instance, or the probable baseball standings next fall, or whether it is fair to keep children out of certain movies, or the age at which it is proper for a girl to start wearing lipstick.)

On all general subjects, naturally, the children hold violently partisan opinions, dictated by what they saw on television, what the teacher said or how Kathy's daddy voted. My husband and I hold opinions which are the result of reasoned, mature thought. Of course, the ending to *our* discussions comes only late at night, after the children are in bed, when my husband and I are still patiently explaining to each other in level voices the complete justice of our own views. (My husband, for instance, favors a weak answering no-trump, although I have time and again explained to him that it is a fallacious bid.)

The family argument usually takes place around the dinner table, somewhere halfway through the main course, when dessert seems impossibly remote beyond the mounds of spinach and the novelty of eating again has largely worn off. Anyone, of course, may commence the fray, but once begun, certain immutable ground rules apply and may not be broken.

Approximately, the ground rules may be stated as:

• The battle must be joined in a spirit of high moral indignation and a correspondingly high voice. In case of an argument on the impersonal level, some intelligent cause for an instance in the subject should be adduced, as "My old teacher made us learn all the parts of the alimentary canal"; or "What *good* is geography, anyway?"

• It is not necessary—is, in fact, reckless—to give anyone else's side of the question.

• The more vivid the detail, the more forceful the complaint. "He hit me and scratched me and pulled my hair and bit me" is clearly a finer many-angled trench to fight from than merely "He hit me."

• Once the arguable premise has been determined, counterattack may consist of flat denial ("I never did"), counteraccusation ("Well, you hit me first") or personal insult ("Anyway, you're nothing but a big baby"). In case of parental involvement, case histories may be admitted into evidence ("Since you are so consistently rude to members of your own family, I can see no reason why we should believe that you are civil to your sister's friends"), and dire prediction may be used as a pseudo threat ("The main part of growing up is the acceptance of responsibility, so a little girl who is going to wear lipstick and fancy shoes will naturally want to be more capable around the house and can therefore plan to wash *and* dry the dishes every night").

• If the father of the family speaks, whether in anger or no, absolute silence must be maintained, although it is not necessary to pay any particular attention to what he is saying.

• If the mother of the family speaks, by heaven everybody had better look alive.

• Any remark like "But gosh, that was way back years ago when you were young" is regarded as dirty tactics.

• The father determines who shall have the floor by shouting "Quiet!" and half-rising from his chair.

• Outside evidence (what Ernie saw, what Kathy said, the probable opinion of old Mrs. Atkins next door) is not allowed as legitimate matter of record, but there is no rule against bringing it up anyway.

• Only the father is permitted to say, "Do as I say, not as I do."

• Anyone who leaves the table in anger must do without candy at bedtime.

• Any apology fairly earned must be delivered as grudgingly as possible ("Yeah, so I *said* I'm sorry"), the mother and father excepted; their apologies must be graceful and complete, to teach the children manners.

• In impersonal arguments, reference books are

referred to ("So go and look it up if you don't believe me") but never referred to.

• Any pronouncement by the mother or the father beginning "From this moment on, every single one of you children will . . ." can be ignored.

• Everyone must choose a side at once, as soon as the issue is brought forward, although it is not necessary to stay on the side you choose if things seem to be going the other way.

In addition to these formal ground rules, certain house rules apply in every family, differing, of course, according to the number of combatants, their several ages and the varying vulnerabilities of the parents. In our family the basic house rules are:

• The father, who is not a man wholly without prejudice, will not suffer disorder. In his presence pictures are to be straightened, books lined evenly on the shelves, silverware correctly placed. It is to be understood that no child of any age will tangle with Daddy on this subject. (The day when Jannie, in a fine white rage, deliberately disarranged all the objects on her father's desk is a day none of us will soon forget.)

• The mother is to be regarded as entirely unreasonable and beyond the reach of logic on such subjects as adequate clothing, riding bicycles in the street, table manners in general and writing Christmas thank-you letters. She is not expected to make any sense with regard to underprotection rather than overprotection.

• The fourteen-year-old son will not permit his privacy to be invaded. Tidy he is not, nor clean, but no one may touch anything that belongs to him.

• The friends of the eleven-year-old daughter may

not be criticized. They are her friends; she herself cannot *stand* that nasty Linda, she is never never going to walk home with Janet again, Millie's behavior is just simply *horrible*; but they are her friends and no one else may cast the second stone.

• The eight-year-old daughter is not to be crossed. She does things in a particular Sally way, and that way is right. Anyone who disagrees is either insane or, at best, hopelessly ignorant. In all of this she strongly resembles her father.

• The five-year-old son is adamant on personal dignity. He will listen, reason, and even consent to stop banging that gun against the wall if he is asked nicely, but at your peril lift him, set him aside, or use force against him because he is small.

• In case the teacher says one thing and the parents another, there is no question in anyone's mind who is right.

Once the ground rules are clearly established (house rules are absorbed by trial and error), the family argument should move quickly and effortlessly. Consider, for example, our family skirmish on the question of our television room, a general sore point anyway.

We have our television set in a small room furnished with a couch, two straight chairs and three walls of bookcases full of books. In front of the couch is a small round table with two ashtrays on it and, in theory, nothing else. The television setup also includes a radio, a phonograph and the attachments for the tape recorder. All four children watch television at some time or other during the usual day, and the couch is convenient for a parental nap after dinner. The room is, in fact, what in a less die-hard family might be called a recreation room, or even a music room, or—stretching a point—a library. One late afternoon recently my husband retired to lie down on the couch and watch the last quarter of the football game before dinner. He came storming out at once announcing that no one, no one, *no one* was ever going to watch television in this house again, or at least only over his dead body. The books had been knocked crooked in all the bookshelves because Barry and Sally had been roughhousing during the commercials. Jannie had left her sewing box and a book borrowed from Linda on one of the chairs. Laurie had been doing his homework in there and the ashtrays were full of torn scraps on which Latin phrases were scrawled, and the floor was covered with little pieces of thread and pencil sharpenings. I myself had left a sweater over the back of the other chair.

As I was clearly one of the sinning parties, I had no choice but to sneak my sweater out fast and attempt to modify the course of justice, at the same time making it clear to the children that Daddy and I were of one mind on everything. I chose to take the unassailable stand that I had told the children and *told* the children to pick up their things, and losing television was no more than they deserved for being so messy; but at the same time, unless something was devised to occupy all four of them during the time I was making dinner, it would very likely be impossible for me to get onto the table any of the small refinements—like deep-dish apple pie— of which my husband is very fond.

My husband said that none of that mattered at all; he would not have the television room left in disorder. Suppose, he demanded fiercely, suppose someone had dropped in to borrow a book? Would we like to have this literate stranger find the books crooked? The ashtrays full of paper? Sweaters lying around everywhere?

No, Laurie said, that was not fairly argued. In the first place, Dad never lent books to anyone because it left spaces in the bookshelves. And Jannie had borrowed the book which caused all the disorder from Kate and he bet that Kate's bookshelves looked even worse.

Jannie said they certainly did *not*; what did Laurie know about Kate's bookshelves, anyway, always thinking he was so smart?

I said that the sweater was mine and I had taken it off because I was going to vacuum the Venetian blinds in the television room; would my husband, I asked hotly, want his literate book-borrower to find the Venetian blinds dusty?

Sally said she had not been roughhousing. Barry had pushed her and she had given him a kind of little small kick.

Barry said she had kicked him *hard*, right *here*, and anyway it was Sally who had fallen off the couch onto the bookcase.

Laurie said if he couldn't do his homework in the television room where *could* he do it? Because how could he work in his room with Jannie playing rock-and-roll on her phonograph all day long?

My husband said now wait a minute, Jannie had every right in the world to play her own phonograph, and in any case rock-and-roll was a legitimate twelve-bar fast blues form.

Laurie said that anyone who could call that junk legitimate didn't know a tenor sax from a clarinet.

His father said that perhaps Laurie with all his education could not count as high as twelve? Because the twelve-bar blues form was exact and only an idiot could ignore it.

Laurie said he could play records that would make Jannie's records sound like a steel mill going full blast.

Sally and Barry began to fidget over their apple pie and their father told them absently to run along and watch television, and he said to Laurie, all right, he would take Jannie's records and show Laurie what was meant by a twelve-bar blues, and in Latin too, if Laurie preferred.

While they were getting out the records I excused myself from the table and went in and straightened up the television room.

There is one argument in our family which is going to be settled out of hand. Five of us think that we should get a new car; there is one holdout who says that we cannot afford it. Four of us think that the new car should be a station wagon; Laurie thinks it should be a convertible, because they are making convertibles now which will hold six and convertibles are the most, man. Three of us think the new station wagon should have four doors instead of two; Barry believes that if there were doors in the back he would fall out. Two of us think the new four-door station wagon should be pink, but Jannie says that that miserable Cheryl has a pink car and it's just *ugly*. One of us thinks that the new pink four-door station wagon is going to have white upholstery and chrome trimmings and look just like a great big luscious strawberry sundae, although Sally prefers raspberry, and by golly that is just the kind of car we are going to get, as soon as I can talk my husband into it.

SHIRLEY JACKSON

When the children are at their most quarrelsome
I have often threatened to scrawl this sentiment
in bold black crayon letters across one dining room
wall:

Ninety percent of the friction of daily life is
caused by tone of voice.

ARNOLD BENNETT

But fiery family wrangling is not the worst form
misunderstanding can take. Fighting is at least a
type of communication! As the children grow into
adolescence we discover that far harder to cope with
is a cold wall of silence.

WORDS FOR A DAUGHTER

Though you have shut me out, your eyes
Betray some wound your speech denies.
You need not fear. I shall remain
Outside. That baffled look of pain
I shall not see, for I must learn
To mask my pity and concern.
And I am proud that you have shown
Courage to face your world alone.

Only remember this: when there
Are times when you have need to share
Your problems, I shall always be
Waiting for you to come to me—

Eager to help you on your way,
Or blunt the sharp edge of dismay.
Your need of me, if you but knew,
Is nothing to my need of you!

ELIZABETH GREY STEWART

When it seems we have lost all touch with a child, we torture ourselves with regrets: was it something we did—or didn't do? And why are things the way they are?

Why did the lamp go out? I shaded it with my cloak
   to save it from the wind, that is why the lamp
   went out.
Why did the flower fade? I pressed it to my heart
   with anxious love, that is why the flower faded.
Why did the stream dry up? I put a dam across it
   to have it for my own use, that is why the
   stream dried up.
Why did the harp string break? I tried to force a
   note that was beyond its power, that is why
   the harp string broke.

RABINDRANATH TAGORE

But truth to tell, no day is entirely dark, now is it? Deep in our hearts we know that somehow everything is going to work out all right. . . . don't we? Just to reinforce that faith, read these two comments over now and then, when the going is very rough indeed. They'll help.

There is never much trouble in any family where the children hope someday to resemble their parents.

WILLIAM LYON PHELPS

Of all the men I have known, I cannot recall one whose mother did her level best for him when he was little who did not turn out well when he grew up.

FRANCES PARKINSON KEYES

Harvest Days

If someone were to plan a testimonial dinner for older mothers and present us with a gold watch, the way industries do when they retire one of their men, at least we would know where we stand. But it doesn't work out that way. It is only gradually that we notice that our children need us less and less, which of course is as it should be, but that doesn't make it easier to bear! Gradually it dawns on us that there is very little left for us to do.

DO AS I TELL YOU!

You have been raised on oranges and milk
and all the vitamins the Lord provides;
your limbs are straight; your skin is soft as silk;
and you have charming curly hair, besides.

With codfish livers and with castile soap,
you have been plied until you look delightful;
you're well supplied with charity and hope;
your temper's sunny if a trifle spiteful.

And now, as you fare blithely forth to slaughter
with those dark eyes some unsuspecting male,
dissemble and be adamant, my daughter;
let no man see you tremble and grow pale.

I did not feed you prunes and carrot juice
so some brash boy could break your heart in splin-
     ters;
nor that you fall so hard, your wits jar loose,
did I preen you summers and zipper you of winters.

Your smile is gay; your nerves are B2 steady;
remember your graceful backbone's braced with cod;
remember suspense makes love extremely heady.
     . . .
I leave the rest to gentlemen—and God.

FRANCES FROST

*These harvest days are a time for facing the fact
that the pattern of our child's character is set—for
good or ill—and that the world is now about to
reap what we have sown.*

ALL YOU HAVE LOVED

All you have loved indubitably lies
Warm in the heart, or sparkles in the eyes:
Bird song at dawns intoxicate with May,

Organs at dusk, slim birches, and the way
A rabbit patterns first snow; color of ocean;
Rain on the roof at midnight, and the motion
Of dancers swaying with unstudied grace;
Old volumes, joy transfiguring a face,
Slow talk in candlelight, and lark spur's blue.
All you have loved is now forever you.

ELAINE V. EMANS

And there is this consolation: magically, many of our problems, and our children's, have resolved themselves.

THE ANSWER

"Dear God," she used to pray, "when I am grown,
Make me as beautiful as sister, please,
With curly hair that's dark and fine and long,
And not a freckle for a boy to tease."
The years could scarcely change the braids of red
To chestnut curls or hide the freckles, quite,
And mirrors did not answer with a dream
Of loveliness until one magic night
When someone said, "You are so beautiful."
Within his eyes she saw her dream come true,
And did not guess that she had found, at last,
The kindest mirror ever woman knew.

ISABELLE BRYANS LONGFELLOW

That's a phase of their growing up we often over-look: the fact that the teen years bring, not just problems, but answers, too.

THE TERRIBLE TEENS

The Terrible Teens are here!

And we've been waiting for most a year
  For the manic moods,
  The frantic "off-foods,"
  The bottomless broods,
  The calling us prudes,
Well-warned, expecting the worst, with fear
That we wouldn't be up to handling the Dear.

Yes, the Terrible Teens are here.

But all they've brought that we can see
  Are pin-up curls,
  And petticoat whirls,
  And the promise of pearls
  As wisdom unfurls,
More fun, more sharing, more love; and, free
From old babyhood cares, we fondly decree

To us The Terrible Teens appear . . . .
  JUST WONDERFUL

                    EMMA GORTON PEIRCE

After all the jests about how hard it is to let teen-agers go out on their own, one would think that surely by now we would have learned to laugh. But can we? Can any of us?

TO A SON AWAY AT COLLEGE

The brightness of the sunlight in your hair
Was like a lamp—now suddenly blown out.

Your laughter through the rooms and on the stair,
Your high exuberance, your boyish shout,
Are silenced, and old distant ivied walls
Have closed you in, where books with their demands
Lay hold upon you, and the future calls,
And draws you forward with persistent hands.
Though the fabric of my mother love is strong,
I would not hold you by a single thread.
Go forward, keep your courage, keep the song
Of living clear, your blood stream clean and red,
Your faith as high as always it has been,
Your values true. . . . But, O dear God, some way
There is a victory I, too, must win
Over the strange fierce loneliness today.

GRACE NOLL CROWELL

*But never think that because they have left our
daily lives, they have really gone from us. Part of
their lives lie in the past, too.*

LETTERS FROM CAMP

Your toys were always soldiers off to battle
And painted ships and tiny dime-store planes—
Your baby hands would never clutch a rattle;
You had no time for wagons or for trains.
A wee tin hat, a gun, a sword to flourish,
A tank to draw behind you on a string—
There were the toys you liked; they helped to nour-
    ish
A climax that I knew the years would bring.

And now that you're away, you are so gentle;
Your letters question—"Is the larkspur tall,
And has the cat new kittens?" Incidental
The things you want to know—so soft and small!
"Mother," you ask, "do you still dress in white—
And eat your evening meal by candlelight?"

MARGARET E. SANGSTER

If memories are a comfort to children, they are the staff of life to mothers—though the memories that haunt us do not always comfort.

COLD NIGHT

At night, when roused by sudden chill,
    Instinctively I start to rise
To see if under covers still
    My children sleep, my anxious eyes
Quest through the dark to where each form
I earlier left, cocooned and warm,
Forgetting that they now are grown
And covering children of their own.

Back to my blanket's warmth I creep:
But not to sleep . . . but not to sleep!

INA STOVALL

No matter how cold and black our loneliness may loom in the empty night, by the practical light of day we know how right it is that they must leave us.

NESTS ARE MADE TO FLY FROM

Now the time is come that you must
be aloft seeking other clouds
and stars to call your own. Once,
I could provide your sky and bring
in suns when moons had been long
overcast; but now the spring is
yours and autumn is my plight.
Could I but keep you for another
fledgling time, I would not; lest
your wings become like weights
or waxen as an Icarus and you
would fear the grandeur of
the turbulent winds.

C. J. MCGRATH, JR.

Not that there aren't adjustments to make; sometimes painful adjustments. Wasn't it Confucius who was asked What is the heaviest burden a man must carry? *and answered* To have no burden. *Of course that philosophy can be carried to extremes. It's a smart mother—or grandmother—who knows when she's well off.*

BIOLOGY, I LOVE YOU

Oh, Friday night is here again,
And now, as oft before,
My grandsons and their sisters
Converge on Grandma's door.
It's time to bake the gingerbread

And wipe the noisy nose,
And let the tots play dress-up
In Grandma's funny clothes.

Come see the tent of Grandma's sheets,
The train of Grandma's chairs!
Come see the bread and jelly
On Grandma's shiny stairs!
Come join the sport; no frown of mine
Tonight shall spoil their fun;
Thank heaven they have two grandmas—
And I'm the other one.

IRENE CARLISLE

That's a wholesome attitude, isn't it? There is nothing more tragic than the awful waste of a woman who has forgotten that she is a woman, and lives only for the children, who of course no longer need nor want that consuming interest. How much more such a mother would do for her children by allowing them to be adults, by allowing them to take care of her a little.

KNITTED SHAWL

She said when we asked her: "Why, nothing, dears,
     at all.
Perhaps a large-print Bible or a little knitted shawl."

We begged her, "Oh, remember!" Because she used
     to tell
Of all that we should bring her when our grown
     world went well—

Gardens full of roses and trips to carry her
Where lovely halls of statues and ancient temples
were

(Gay feet and restless, that never could run free,
Because of our hands clinging to hand and breast
and knee!)

But we who could recall her, so young and tired and
gay
With long, wild, girlish longings for things she could
not say—

All that we could bring her forever now at all
Was just a large-print Bible and a little knitted
shawl.

MARGARET WIDDEMER

But an entirely new breed of grandmother is appearing on the American scene these days—have you noticed?

THEY WRITE OF MOTHERS . . . .

They write of mothers with snowy hair,
    And faces old and wrinkled,
And gentle, folded, careworn hands
    That oft with tears are sprinkled.
I wish some one would write a song
    For mothers young and gay,
With well-kept hair and skin and hands
    And tears they've dashed away.

MARION BEARD

Yet, however excellent may be our adjustment to our new role, still the children and their interests are our lives, to a large extent.

MOTHER

Her mind is a library, where Dickens, Scott,
And the Harvard Classics lie dusty, forgot;
But where certain small books may always be had,
Strange-titled volumes that make her heart glad:
    Must fix Jim's shirt,
    Buy Helen's skirt,
    Shoes for Dad . . .

Her heart is a music room, where Schubert's, Lack's
And Beethoven's works lie in cobwebby stacks;
But where songs well-dusted are always near,
Funny little songs, whose names are so queer:
    Little Helen's "why,"
    Jim's twinkly eyes,
    Dad, my dear . . .

Her fingers are a game room, where, now unused,
Lie tennis balls, whist cards, the old organ, bruised;
But where never a thought is given those,
Because she's a wonder at new games she knows:
    Favorite desserts,
    Ironing shirts,
    Mending clothes . . .

Her eyes are an observatory, where Mercury,
Mars, Venus, Neptune are too distant to see;
But where certain bright stars make all others dim,
Her oddly named planets that make her eyes brim:

Dad,
Helen,
Jim . . .

ETHEL BARNETT DE VITO

*Even if all we have is the tenuous thread of letters
to which we can cling, they are enough.*

THE LETTERS

The neighbors couldn't understand, somehow,
That, though alone, she was not lonely now.
Nice folk, the neighbors, if they'd let her be;
But they blamed her boy for going off to sea.
They scorned the lovely gifts he sent:
That shiny string of bright-pink pearls from Ghent,
The yellow crepe-de-chine shawl from Shanghai
(That was the time she couldn't help but cry),
The fan with painted roses from Peking—
Strange how Miz Collins' well-meant words should
    sting:
"All I can say is, ain't that like a man,
Here you are freezin' and he sends a fan!
Here when food and clothing are cruel needs,
He only thinks to send a shawl and beads;
Here when you sit alone these long, cold nights,
He thinks he's done his duty if he writes!"

But they didn't see the letters that he wrote—
Letters from foreign ports or from the boat,
Telling of all the strange things that he saw,
Wonderful letters starting: "Dearest Ma,"

Letters that all said: "Someday you and me
Will have a small white cottage near the sea."
Reading these words by lamplight, that was how
She was alone but never lonely now.
And some nights when she'd just received a note,
She'd clasp the bright-pink pearls around her throat,
Put on the lovely yellow silken shawl,
And take the painted fan down from the wall,
Then stand at the old cracked mirror for a while,
Till, flushed and bright-eyed, smiling a little smile,
She'd sit at the table always set for one,
To write a letter starting: "Dearest Son."

ETHEL BARNETT DE VITO

*These can be the richest, the warmest, the most re-
warding days of all, if we live them to the fullest.
Now we can know our children in a deeper way than
was possible while they were very small. Now they
are having children of their own; now they are feeling the oneness that links them with all the parents
who went before them down the road they are walking. Our work is done, and all we have to give our
children, we have now given.*

A wise woman once said to me: "There are only two
lasting bequests we can hope to give our children.
One of these is roots; the other, wings."

HODDING CARTER

*The most beautiful expression I know of the desire
of every mother to leave a legacy for her children,*

is the often-reprinted The Last Will. They say the man who wrote these lovely lines was a bachelor. That's hard to believe. Surely they sound as though they sprang from the heart of a mother.

THE LAST WILL

Item: And first, I give to good fathers and mothers, but in trust for their children, nevertheless, all good little words of praise and all quaint pet names, and I charge said parents to use them justly, but generously, as the needs of their children shall require.

Item: I leave to children exclusively, but only for the life of their childhood, all and every the dandelions of the fields and the daisies thereof, with the right to play among them freely, according to the custom of children, warning them at the same time against the thistles. And I devise to children the yellow shores of creeks and the golden sands beneath the waters thereof, with the dragon-flies that skim the surface of said waters, and the odors of the willows that dip into said waters, and the white clouds that float over giant trees.

And I leave to children the long, long days to be merry in, in a thousand ways, and the Night and the Moon and the train of the Milky Way to wonder at, but subject, nevertheless, to the rights hereinafter given to lovers; and I give to each child the right to choose a star that shall be his.

Item: I devise to boys jointly all the useful idle fields
and commons where ball may be played, and
all the snow-clad hills where one may coast,
and all the streams and ponds where one may
skate, to have and to hold the same for the
period of their boyhood. And all the woods,
with squirrels and whirling birds and echoes
and strange noises; and all the distant places
which may be visited, together with the ad-
ventures there found, I do give to said boys
to be theirs. And I give to said boys each his
own place at the fireside at night, with all
pictures that may be seen in the burning
wood or coal, to enjoy without let or hin-
drance and without any incumbrance of
cares.

Item: To lovers I devise their imaginary world,
with whatever they may need, as the stars
of the sky, the red, red roses by the wall, the
snow of the hawthorne, the sweet strains of
music, or aught else they may desire to figure
to each other the beauty of their love.

Item: To young men jointly, being joined in a
brave, mad crowd, I devise and bequeath all
boisterous, inspiring sports of rivalry. I give
to them the disdain of weakness and un-
daunted confidence in their own strength.
Though they are rude and rough, I leave to
them alone the power of making lasting
friendships and of possessing companions,
and to them exclusively I give all merry
songs and brave choruses to sing.

Item: And to those who are no longer children, or youths, or lovers, I leave Memory, and I leave to them the volumes of the poems of Burns and Shakespeare, and of other poets, if there are others, to the end that they may live the old days over again, freely, fully, without tithe or diminution; and to those who are no longer children, or youths, or lovers, I leave, too, the knowledge of what a rare, rare world it is.

WILLISTON FISH

INDEX OF AUTHORS

INDEX OF TITLES

INDEX OF FIRST LINES